THE WOW FACTORY

Creating a Customer Focus
Revolution in Your Business

THE WOW FACTORY

Creating a Customer Focus
Revolution in Your Business

Paul Levesque

IRWIN
Professional Publishing

Chicago • Bogotá • Boston • Buenos Aires • Caracas
London • Madrid • Mexico City • Sydney • Toronto

Senior sponsoring editor: Cynthia A. Zigmund
Project editor: Jane Lightell
Production manager: Pat Frederickson
Designer: Laurie J. Entringer/David Corona Design
Art manager: Kim Meriwether
Compositor: David Corona Design
Typeface: 11/13 Palatino
Printer: Quebecor Printing—Kingsport

Library of Congress Cataloging-in-Publication Data

Levesque, Paul
    The WOW factory: creating a customer focus revolution in your
business / Paul Levesque.
        p.   cm.
    ISBN 0-7863-0386-7
    1. Consumer satisfaction. 2. Customer service 3. Organizational
effectiveness. I. Title.
HF5415.3.L474   1995
658.8'12—dc20
                                                        94–31410

No profit grows where is no pleasure ta'en.

—William Shakespeare

For Aileen Levesque, my mom,
who taught me all about exceeding expectations.

Preface

Ours is a society that often invests more effort in the treatment of symptoms than in the eradication of the maladies they represent. Everyone knows what to take for a headache, even if no one has much of an idea what may be *causing* the headaches.

Most businesses today share a host of common symptoms: sagging profits, demotivated employees, a lack of clear organizational direction, a shrinking customer base, plenty of internal conflict and disagreement, an overall feeling of futility and discouragement. Many are taking something for these symptoms: total quality management (TQM), continuous quality improvement (CQI), quality function deployment (QFD), self-directed teams, employee empowerment, process reengineering. These are all highly effective pain relievers. I know; I've been dispensing many of them myself for years.

This book is the product of over a decade of close personal collaboration with businesses and organizations of all types and sizes, all of them struggling to overcome these very symptoms. The fundamental question it attempts to answer is, if these are the symptoms, what is the disease? Is there some way we can begin addressing root causes?

There is. All these symptoms are simply the outward manifestation of something inward that is lacking in most businesses. That something is customer focus. Not customer *service*, not customer *relations*, not a set of guidelines or behaviors that some of the employee population is expected to adhere to some of the time (when interacting directly with customers); customer *focus* is a whole state of mind that has a direct bearing on every decision every person in the organization will make every minute of every day.

So, if this is the key, why aren't more businesses bypassing all the fancy buzzwords and just setting out to develop greater *customer focus*, pure and simple? Why aren't they positioning all those other components as subordinate elements, to be drawn upon as necessary to support the customer focus initiative? I've discovered over the years that there are two reasons why most businesses still aren't making a serious, conscious effort to become more customer focused. They're lacking two very important things:

1. A *reason* for becoming more customer focused (which is to say, they simply haven't yet caught on; they haven't made the connection).

2. A *method* for becoming more customer focused (which is to say, they wouldn't know where to begin anyway).

The purpose of the book you're holding is to provide you with both the reason and the method for making your business more customer focused. It's aimed at any business in any industry—from a one-person garage operation to a multinational corporation—that finds itself suffering from some or all of the symptoms listed above.

Part I (Chapters 1 through 4) summarizes the best reasons for shifting your organization's focus toward the customer. Not only can doing so improve bottom-line results, it can also make working in your business more satisfying and fun for everyone involved. Employees stand to benefit as much as customers do. Part I is the section to turn to for inspiration and awareness, for a better grasp of the whole customer focus issue and all its implications.

Part II (Chapters 5 through 12) outlines a step-by-step process for guiding your team through a creative customer focus brainstorming session. This is the nuts-and-bolts how-to section of the book. It shows you how to help your team understand and begin applying the three core principles of customer focus. Here a wealth of innovative ideas for giving your business a powerful competitive advantage will be generated and recorded.

Though the techniques outlined in this book are powerful, they should not be thought of as replacements for other kinds of specialized disciplines like those listed above. Instead, customer focus provides the perfect *context* for the others. It raises awareness and highlights potential sources of customer dissatisfaction that might otherwise remain hidden; the specialized disciplines can then be called upon to correct those problems for which the solutions are not immediately obvious. It becomes easier for employees to support a variety of improvement approaches if they are all seen to be simply components of a single, bigger, all-encompassing effort: the need to become more customer focused.

Acknowledgments

A book like this cannot be written in isolation. I owe a tremendous debt of gratitude to the hundreds of businesses around the world with whom I've had the opportunity to play and work, to experiment, to refine ideas and approaches, to document successes. My sincerest thanks to every one of you.

Thanks, too, to Rob Ell, who opened up the world of storyboarding to me back in the early days, and to Art McNeil for trusting me enough to hand me the keys to his magic kingdom and to the many doors of opportunity connected to it.

A special thanks, as well, to my NPA partners, Sid and Tom Tomkins, for their unfailing encouragement and support.

Last, I must acknowledge the immeasurable contribution my friend and business partner Andy Parisien has made to this book—and to my whole life: over 30 years of close friendship, characterized predominantly by an endless, rollicking, roaring cascade of shared laughter. Thank you, Andre, for helping me learn to see things in that unique Mack & Charter way of yours.

Paul Levesque

Contents

Trademark

Post-it™ Notes is a trademark of 3M.

THE CUSTOMER FOCUS CONCEPT

Chapter One

What's Our Primary Business Objective?

A LITTLE LESS CHANGE WOULD BE NICE FOR A CHANGE

In Stanley Kubrick's 1968 film *2001: A Space Odyssey*, there's a scene in which a commercial shuttle-type spacecraft is making its way to an orbiting space station. Proudly emblazoned on the ship's fuselage is the familiar Pan Am logo. Remember Pan Am? In an earlier Kubrick movie, *Dr. Strangelove*, tensions between the United States and the Soviet Union reach cataclysmic proportions. Remember the Soviet Union? Remember the Berlin Wall? The Threat of International Communism? The LP? Remember *Future Shock*, the (now almost ancient) book that warned that the pace of change in our world and in our lives was liable to start getting a bit hairy?

Adapt or perish—it's the law of survival. In a changing world, either we change to conform as best we can to the new circumstances or we attempt to resist the tide of change until eventually, inevitably, it sweeps us away. Have you had a chance to look at this morning's newspaper yet? It's like a daily casualty list. Take a look. Organizations, institutions, entire societies being swept away every day. Check out the business section. How many enterprises frighteningly similar to your own have bitten the dust within the

past 24 hours? Turn to the front page. Insurrection everywhere. Revolt, rebellion. Now back to the business section.
Customers flocking to alternate suppliers. Declining market
share. Dwindling sales figures. Lay the pages side by side—
unhappy constituencies putting governments out of business, unhappy customers putting suppliers out of business.
The specific manifestations may differ, but the basic phenomenon is the same.

And what is this global phenomenon that's generating so
much unhappiness and shaking things up around the world?
It boils down to *rising expectations*. Everybody's expecting
more and better from everybody else and becoming more
dissatisfied (and assertive) when it's not forthcoming. And
what's driving these expectations skyward in the first place?
Information—the mere knowledge that better possibilities
exist, that better conditions prevail elsewhere. When the
politically oppressed begin getting a clearer picture of life
under democratic rule, they find they can tolerate their
oppression no more. When angry, frustrated customers
discover that a new supplier may be able to provide higher
levels of satisfaction, they pull up stakes and transfer their
business without hesitation. In either case, all the old loy-
alties disappear with startling swiftness the moment a potentially better alternative presents itself. If we are
determined not to become the party abandoned in favor of
the better alternative, then we have no other choice than to
become the better alternative. We adapt, or we perish—which
is to say, alas, we must change.

ARE WE IN ENOUGH PAIN YET?

Any change—even when it's a transition to something
better—has some pain associated with it. There's the time
it's going to take, time we simply do not have and cannot
possibly spare. There's the money it's going to cost, which

is even worse because, let's face it, while we probably *could* free up some time in a pinch, it's *money* we absolutely can't get our hands on no matter how hard we try. Then there's the possibility that our change effort will fail and we'll end up looking foolish (which, of course, is a lot worse than the time and money, both of which, let's face it, we could probably scrape up without too much trouble if we really had to).

The way it usually works out is that we won't willingly undertake change until the pain of *not* doing so becomes great enough to exceed the pain we anticipate from the change itself. And by then, of course, it's often too late—which helps explain many of the new names on the daily casualty lists. Note, incidentally, that in the "to-change-or-not-to-change" debate, the tendency is always to weigh pain against pain, the misery of the way things are against the misery of moving toward something better. The hypothetical benefits to come are by no means guaranteed, so they don't even enter into the equation. (Keep that in mind when you try to generate some enthusiasm among your colleagues or employees. Your glorious depiction of the utopia-to-be will go a mile over their heads; their glassy stares will mean, "Cut the flowers and just tell us how badly this is going to hurt." You've got to prove to them, as you did to yourself, that *not* going after the utopia will ultimately hurt even more.) Let's assume, then, just for the fun of it, that you have picked up this book and have read this far because you are prepared to willingly undertake some change in the way you conduct your business. I'm going to further assume that you haven't delayed making this decision beyond any point of no return. The question then becomes, "What do we need to change first?"

Our starting point should involve taking a hard, critical look at the way we think about our business. We need to ask ourselves where we tend to focus our attention and our energies—and whether we need to *shift* our focus elsewhere.

The purpose of this book is to show businesses how to develop a greater customer focus. But what *is* customer focus, exactly? What does it actually look like? One of the quickest ways to discover what customer focus looks like is to observe what its *absence* looks like.

PLEASE DON'T BOTHER ME—I'VE GOT A JOB TO DO

High above the Atlantic, the flight attendant asked me what kind of wine I wanted with my dinner. I told her I'd prefer mineral water instead. "Oh dear," she said with a pained expression, "well, I'll have to bring you that later. Right now I'm in the middle of Meal Service." She could not bring me my beverage because she was busy. She had a job to do. Her job was serving meals. (As opposed to, say, serving passengers.)

During a two-week stay in Chicago, I repeatedly arrived at my hotel room in the early evening just as the attendant was restocking my mini-bar. "Have you noticed," I asked him on one occasion, "that for the past several days all you ever find on my countertop are the two little teeny-weeny Diet Pepsi bottles this mini-bar supplies, both empty, and nothing else?"

"Yes sir," he smiled, transferring two fresh teeny-weeny bottles of Diet Pepsi from his cart to the small refrigerator.

"Wouldn't this tend to suggest that out of all the different items in my mini-bar, the only item I am personally interested in is Diet Pepsi?"

"Well . . . yes, sir."

"So what do you think would happen if one day, just for laughs, you were to put *four* teeny-weeny bottles of Diet Pepsi in there? Think you'd find four empties the next day?"

"Probably," he chuckled, locking up the mini-bar with the regulation plastic seal.

"So why don't you do it?"

He turned and gave me a troubled look. "Oh, I can't do that, sir," he said. He held up a sheet of paper listing the contents of the mini-bar: two of everything. "I can only replace what gets used up."

A man with a job to do, his job was filling mini-bars (very different from, for example, filling guest requests).

> **The scene:** virtually every record store in your neighborhood and mine.

> **The setup:** waist-high bins of discounted compact discs strategically positioned near the front of the store to encourage perusal of the titles printed on the spines of the disc boxes.

> **The problem:** perusal is difficult and tedious because *upside-down disc spines are indiscriminately mixed with right-side-up spines.*

> **The result:** shoppers browse in the discount bins only until their necks tire of the back-and-forth twisting and turning required to read the tiny print (usually in less than a minute) and then abandon the effort and move along.

The reason this preposterous situation exists in practically every record store in the civilized world: someone on staff was given a job to do. Their job was to transfer discounted discs from the regular bins to a new location: inside the discount bins (instead of, for example, to an *alternate* new location: inside customers' homes).

You stand next to an abandoned cash register in a department store, your selected item of merchandise in one hand, your cold hard cash in the other. The sales clerk is 12 feet away, putting the finishing touches on a pyramid-shaped display of items identical to the one you hold in your hand.

You catch her casting a split-second glance in your direction; she has seen you but proceeds with her display as if she has not. You're just going to have to wait, because right now she has a *job* to do. Her job is to display these items in an attractive manner so people will want to buy them. Her supervisor has already reprimanded her for taking so long on this very important task. Eventually you put your unbought item down and put your unspent money away as you head for the exit. The sales clerk steps back from her display to see how it looks from a distance, tipping her head this way and that to size it up from every angle. She knows her supervisor is very fussy and will give her a hard time unless it's just so.

Customer focus—just about everywhere you look, it's not there. In the town of Sarnia, Ontario, a shopping center installed *parking meters* in its parking lot. (Presumably this was the result of someone being given a job to do: increase revenues.) The vast, empty parking lot reminded me of a deserted drive-in theater, with meters on posts replacing loudspeakers on posts. Signs printed on each table in the food area of this same complex read, "Thank you for your patronage. No loitering." (I wish they wouldn't beat around the bush that way. Why not just come right out and say, "Either buy something immediately or get out!")

The signs and notices on display in a business establishment tell a great deal about where the business places its focus. I always like seeing empty parking spaces close to the front door that are designated Reserved for Management, while employees and customers must squeeze themselves into whatever space remains as best they can. This sign was posted on the wall near the "Please Wait to Be Seated" sign in a well-known deli in one of Toronto's trendiest neighborhoods: "If you want gravy on your french fries, please say so in advance—we're not mind readers!" (Diners hadn't even made it to their seats yet, and they were already being warned to smarten up.) Particularly appealing are the crudely hand-lettered homemade signs—"Don't touch unless you intend to buy." "Don't read the books—we're not a library." "Don't block the doorway." "Move to the back of the bus." "Wipe your feet." "No pets allowed." "No credit." "No personal checks." "No refunds." "No substitutions."—all of which help us quickly conclude that doing business with these businesses will be "no picnic." In an outlet for a famous chain of submarine sandwiches, atop the self-serve soft-drink dispenser: "No free refills." (I especially like the way this one reminds patrons of the competitor down the street where refills *are* free! Another equally effective way to do promotion work for competitors is to pipe radio programming over the in-house sound system, complete with attention-grabbing commercials for the competition.)

When businesses replace paper towel dispensers in their public washrooms with those hot-air dryers everyone hates, when they replace mustard and ketchup dispensers with those little unopenable plastic packets that send the contents flying and waste as much as they use, when bottled or canned cola is replaced by that black sludge with the paint-thinner taste that emerges from fountain machines, the underlying motive usually involves cutting costs, increasing margins, making more money. We've somehow become a society of businesses dedicated to the belief that the way to increase profits is to frustrate, insult, reprimand, and ultimately alienate our customers.

Everyone's got a "job" to do. Every worker in every business is caught up in his or her daily tasks, coping with his or her crisis-du-jour. They've all got too much on their plate and too little time to get it all done. A stranger suddenly comes wandering into their workplace—a customer, looking lost and confused. Who's going to abandon their assigned task and take the time to approach this poor soul and find out what the problem is? All eyes are lowered; maybe he'll just go away. *I* certainly can't do anything for him—I've got to get this huge "Let's Start Helping Our

Customers" poster ready for tomorrow's big Customer Service meeting or my boss'll *kill* me! I've got a *job* to do.

Most workers in most businesses today are task focused. Many have lost their ability to make a connection between the all-important task at hand and those nameless, faceless strangers called customers who drift in and our of their immediate landscape and find so many tiresome ways of preventing them from getting the job done.

This lost ability to connect our jobs with our customers becomes a double tragedy. It leads to consistent customer dissatisfaction, which ultimately puts businesses out of business and cripples our economy. It also makes working for a living a painful experience. It fills our workdays with an endless succession of dreary, pointless tasks. It generates stress and bitterness and uncertainty that spill over into our personal worlds and contaminate our whole way of life. As a society, we've somehow forgotten just how satisfying and rewarding "being in business" can be. It's time we change the way we think.

WHAT BUSINESS ARE WE REALLY IN?

To successfully adapt to the changing reality of your marketplace, you need to step well back from the day-to-day details of your operation for a moment and reconsider an extremely fundamental question: *what, at the most basic level imaginable, is the primary objective of your business enterprise in the first place?* When you begin each new workday, what's in the back of your mind as the ultimate purpose behind all the different tasks and activities that will take up your time and attention? What's it all for? In the grand overall scheme of things, what's it all intended to accomplish? Review the list of possible answers below; use a pen or pencil to circle the number next to the one that most closely approximates how you would answer the question. (By definition, there can be only one primary objective.)

My Primary Business Objective:

1. Acquire more customers.
2. Make more money.
3. Make employees happier.
4. Make customers happier.
5. Make work more fun.

There is, of course, no single right or wrong answer to this question. But if you selected the second answer (as most people do, incidentally), it means you may have a considerably more difficult time *achieving* your objective than if you'd chosen any of the others. Unless, of course, you're prepared to begin changing the way you think.

Read the next few paragraphs very carefully; they divulge one of the best-kept secrets in business today.

In any enterprise, when increasing the level of profit becomes the primary objective, profits usually suffer. Businesses going under will emphatically protest that their extremely determined efforts to remain profitable seem tragically to be to no avail. The real tragedy is that most won't discover in time how their plight may be worsening precisely *because* their prime focus is on profits, instead of where it should be.

Take another look at the five possible answers to the question above. They are linked in a curious way—achieving any one of them will cause one or more of the others to be achieved as well. If answer 1 is realized, for example, there's a good chance that answer 2 will also be realized as a result, along, perhaps, with answer 5. An intriguing question then becomes, which of the listed objectives, if met, has the potential of causing the greatest number of remaining objectives to be met? These are all very desirable objectives; if one seems to do a better job of meeting all the others (including answer 2), wouldn't it make sense to make *that* one our primary objective?

One of the five does stand out in this regard. Review the list, see if you agree. Of all five objectives, only answer 4, if met, virtually guarantees that all the remaining objectives would be met as a result. Practically no one selects answer 4 the first time around, and yet no other business objective has as great a potential to accomplish as many positive things—including increasing the levels of profit.

If you are truly serious about making your enterprise successful, then your primary business objective *must* become to *produce happy customers*. Beginning immediately, this must take precedence over every other consideration. You're not actually in the shoe business at all, or the pizza business, or the software business, or whatever business heading you happen to be listed under in the Yellow Pages; you're in, to borrow a phrase from the advertising of a car rental company, the *pleasing* business. Shoes or pizzas or whatever you consider your basic product or service to be— these are simply *tools* you happen to use in the manufacture of your real product: happy customers.

The true measure of your success in the marketplace is not your profit statement; all kinds of misleading factors can be pushing that up or down at any given point in time. Fire half your staff tomorrow morning and the sudden drop in overhead will make your bottom line look terrific—for a while. But if your real product is happy customers, everything you and all your co-workers do is (or should be) geared to the creation of this one thing. Your success is therefore measured by how happy your customers are (the quality of your product) and by the extent to which their numbers are growing (the quantity of your product). It's really quite simple: whoever creates the most happy customers wins.

The people running most businesses today are clearly profit focused. Many have lost altogether their ability to see how this emphasis on profits shifts everyone's attention away from the customer, which sooner or later is bound to cause profits to dwindle.

Those (few) businesses that have learned to concentrate on creating happy customers tend to generate the kind of profits that make the competition sick with envy. Nor are higher profits the only pleasant by-product of happy customers; employee morale and pride are also heightened. Workers derive far greater satisfaction from their jobs when customers routinely present them with bouquets and letters of commendation, instead of coming at them after dark in the parking lot with torches and packs of snarling dogs. That's why, for example, most young people would prefer to work at McDonald's, even though they know they'll be kept busy, rather than at Biff's Burger Grease-A-Rama down the block, where for about the same pay they'd barely have to do anything at all, since Biff's is *never* busy. And when employee satisfaction increases, absenteeism and turnover decrease—cost savings that go right to the bottom line and make the profit picture even rosier.

To successfully adapt to the changing realities of our marketplace, a good starting point involves redefining what the basic objective of our business really is or should be. If the workers are task focused and the managers are profit focused, who's left to be *customer* focused?

And if the creation of happy customers is to become our primary business objective, we need to be very certain we can answer the question, "What is it that *makes* customers happy?" Chapter 2 offers some food for thought on this question.

Snappy Summary

▶ The primary objective of any business is (or should be) to produce happy customers.

▶ Customer expectations are at an all-time high—and continue to rise.

▶ A strong customer focus can generate higher profits than a strong focus on profits alone.

▶ Most workers are task focused, most managers are profit focused; who's left to be *customer* focused?

Chapter Two

What Are We Really Selling?

WHAT DO CUSTOMERS *EXPECT,* ANYWAY?

Suppose I'm in the market for a new TV set. Suppose I happen to know that there are two stores, each about the same distance from my home, that sell good TVs. They carry different *brands* of TVs, but I've read the consumer magazines and I happen to know that these competing brands are of comparably high quality; also, both offer virtually identical features at the same price. On what basis, then, will I decide where to buy my new TV? Well, I may decide on the basis of which store has the most parking space. Or which is open for business at the times most convenient for me. Or which has the friendliest, most helpful sales staff. Or which has the most attractive returns-and-refunds policy. And so on.

The important thing to note in all of this is that parking space or business hours or friendliness are factors that have absolutely nothing to do with TV sets. In effect, I'll be selecting which TV to buy not on the basis of TV-related factors but rather on the basis of customer-treatment–related factors.

And there, at its simplest, is the new reality of customer expectations. When our parents splurged on the luxury of a TV set, they shopped around for the best price or the best picture quality; when it's time for us to pick up a second or third set, we shop around for the easiest parking. A lot has changed in just a few decades.

This is not to suggest that competing on price is no longer a useful business strategy, nor is it meant to imply that superior quality can no longer give businesses a competitive advantage. Indeed, if space permitted, we might explore at considerable length the subtle ways in which both of these time-honored approaches do or do not still apply to today's business realities. But the important issue is that both of these considerations are increasingly being eclipsed by something bigger, something more fundamental, something with deeper implications. And the reasons for this eclipse are not all that mysterious.

Consider the three little words *Made in Japan*. For about the first half of the century, these words were pretty widely understood to mean "cheap junk"; today many interpret the words *Made in America* to mean an "inferior copy of a Japanese original." The worldwide quest for quality that began in Japan after World War II has driven up customer expectations to the point where the quality and affordability of basic goods and services are increasingly considered givens. Today, businesses that can't consistently deliver high quality at a low price simply don't survive. They disappear from the playing field. It becomes more and more difficult to distinguish between those still in the game when they're all delivering comparable quality at comparable prices. The *differences* in quality and in price, which were once significant enough to make the selection of a supplier relatively easy, are becoming so slight that their power as competitive differentiators is diminishing daily.

So how do customers currently select their suppliers? On what basis are businesses currently compared to each other? The choice is now often made on the basis of how a given business *adds value* to its products and services. And increasingly, the extent to which a business can add value is directly proportional to the extent to which it is customer focused.

For our own business to become more customer focused, we must begin by recognizing this simple truth about customer expectations: *customers expect us to strive very hard to make them happy every step of the way.* Each time an aspect of the total experience meets that expectation, we have added value in the customer's eyes. Conversely, each aspect of the experience that disappoints the customer detracts from the value of doing business with us, however flawless our basic product itself may be on its own. We may think that what we're selling is our so-called basic product (furniture, or health care, or pizzas, or whatever), but the customer sees it differently. From the customer's point of view, we're actually selling the *whole experience* of doing business with us.

The total experience is made up of many elements: how many times the phone rings before it is answered, how long one is kept waiting at the counter, how accurate the order is, how carefully the goods are packed, whether delivery deadlines are met, whether the premises are spotless, whether forms are easy to use, whether merchandise is easy to find—the list goes on and on. And yet it is precisely on the basis of this complex, multifaceted total experience that we are compared to our competitors. Whoever serves up the best total experience (and therefore creates the most happy customers) wins. A small (but growing) minority of businesses are finding ways to consciously tailor the whole experience to the needs and expectations of their customers—to become totally customer focused, in other words. These organizations tend to prosper, even in troubled economic times. To these businesses customers migrate, leaving the rest to wither and wind up on the daily casualty lists.

How customer-focused businesses add value can take on enough importance in customers' eyes to eventually become an indistinguishable part of the basic product itself. Serving hot meals aboard commercial aircraft, for example, must at one time have seemed the epitome of extravagant customer pampering; today, frequent flyers choosing between competing airlines offering comparable schedules, fares, and aircraft routinely favor one airline over another strictly on the basis of a preference for its food. Like it or not, many airlines that have always thought of themselves as being in the aviation business are discovering that they're actually in the *restaurant* business: a value-added extra has become a key part of their basic product. The irony is that many of these same airlines remain blissfully unaware of their customers' preferences and so are ruthlessly slashing expenses—including fancy meals—rather than looking for creative low-cost ways to add value to the flying experience.

THE WOW FACTOR

We might as well face it, customer expectations are going to continue to rise, with or without our help. Therefore, as more and more businesses learn to deliver satisfaction at every stage of the total experience, customers will quickly come to think of this higher level of satisfaction as just one more given. So how, then, will businesses compete?

The answer may require another adjustment in the way we think. The traditional definition of customer satisfaction has always revolved around the notion of meeting expectations. Thus, to increase the level of satisfaction it became necessary to increase the number of expectations that were being met—once they were *all* met, the customer would be fully satisfied. Well, this is a fine and worthy goal that by all means should be pursued. But what if we can do better than merely "satisfying" our customers? What if we could blow their socks off?

Think of a real-life situation in which you, as a customer, encountered a succession of pleasant surprises, big and small, at every turn. Does the word *satisfaction* adequately describe what you were feeling at the time? And were your expectations merely "met" in that instance? When I ask these questions in my Customer Focus workshops, participants typically use words like *delighted* and *thrilled* to describe their feelings in such cases and add without hesitation that their expectations were definitely *exceeded*. They experienced the "wow" factor.

The encouraging news is that while the wow factor can boost customer happiness significantly, it usually doesn't represent a proportionately significant outlay of extra effort; in fact, once we've done whatever needs to be done to *satisfy* our customers, we frequently need only add some very small—almost insignificant—touches to transform satisfaction into delight.

To illustrate, I'm sometimes given, as an example of the wow factor, the practice of flight attendants aboard some airlines to address their passengers by name: "Would you care for another beverage, Mr. Stamplecoskie?" "Can I get you a pillow, Mr. Stamplecoskie?" Interestingly, those who cite this as an example don't seem overly impressed with the fact that the same airline managed to send a couple of hundred people hurtling down a paved roadway at such dangerously high speed that their slender hotel-room-on-wheels (packed with enough explosive fuel to blow everybody to smithereens) actually left the ground altogether and took to the sky, crossed the continent at some impossible speed, and at the other end began rushing toward the ground nose first, yet was able at the last second to level off and gently deposit the whole works safely on another paved roadway—and most miraculous of all, was even able to arrange for quite a few of the passengers' bags to show up at the destination as well. All of this, of course, is a given; it is expected. But being addressed by *name*—wow! The wow factor usually represents very little things, but things that from the customer's point of view often make a very big difference.

Some businesses become so impressed with the power of the wow factor as a means of creating happy customers that they decide to focus their energies on that element alone. Rather than first satisfying customers by meeting their expectations and then adding a wow factor element to "plus" the experience, they'll fumble their way through the preliminary stages and then try to counteract any resulting dissatisfaction with some sort of splashy wow factor finish. This is invariably a fatal mistake. It's like placing a lavishly ornamented picture frame around a tattered, shabby piece of blank canvas and expecting people to happily pay for the privilege of gazing at the result. Though the lit candles atop a birthday cake never fail to elicit an appreciative chorus of oohs and aahs, those same lit candles *without* the cake, stuck into a dirty piece of corrugated cardboard all by themselves and presented thus to the recipient, somehow just aren't likely to carry quite the same impact. Similarly, Mr. Stamplecoskie's high regard for the airline is liable to suffer somewhat when he discovers that the flight attendant is addressing him by name for the sole purpose of advising him to place his head between his knees, since the engines have failed and the plane's about to crash.

Another common mistake is to believe that customers need only be wowed once and they'll be hooked for life. On the contrary, even the most impressive service achievements are a pleasant surprise only the first time; they will be expected thereafter. That which blows customers' socks off today will simply be meeting their expectations tomorrow. If a competitor finds ways to *exceed* those expectations tomorrow, that competitor promptly becomes the better alternative, and we can start kissing our customers good-bye. To sustain the wow factor, to transform our business into an ongoing "Wow Factory," we must continuously upgrade the experience. (Fortunately, as we'll soon see, doing so can actually turn out to be a lot of fun.)

CUSTOMER SERVICE VERSUS CUSTOMER FOCUS

With the growing appreciation of the importance of customer service in some business quarters, there might understandably be some confusion around the relationship between the concepts of customer service and customer focus.

The terms are not, in fact, interchangeable—the former is really a *subset* of the latter. It may help to think of customer service as the quality of the treatment customers receive during *points of contact* with the supplier. (Any kind of interaction, whether face to face, over the telephone, through the mail, via fax machine, teleconference, smoke signals, or jungle drums qualifies as a point of contact.) Customer focus considers the quality of the *total customer experience*. This includes not only our points of contact with customers but also the very nature of the basic products and services we offer, the policies and procedures we follow in conducting our business, the decor within our business premises, the hours during which we'll be open for business, the extent to which our employees will be empowered to take initiatives and make decisions on the customer's behalf, and an endless conglomeration of other elements that all have a bearing on what customers will ultimately experience when they do business with us. Customer service is a key component of customer focus, but it's not the whole picture.

Fictional case in point: Richard has been out late at a Smedley Falls night spot, entertaining a prospective new client. He doesn't get back to his hotel room at the Meaty

Ocher Inn until after 2 in the morning and is grateful that his presentation to the executive team the next day isn't scheduled until after lunch and that he can therefore catch a little extra sleep. He carries his own travel alarm clock wherever he goes but is delighted not to have to set it on this occasion.

Richard is startled out of a deep sleep at 6:30 in the morning by the sudden screech of loud, tinny music mere inches from his ear. At first, in the darkness, he's bewildered—where is he, and what on earth is that racket right beside him? He remembers that he checked into a hotel the day before; the noise is from the bedside clock radio, presumably set to go off at this hour by the room's previous occupant. Richard fumbles for the bedside lamp so he can figure out how to silence the howling radio. No light from the lamp. He'd forgotten—the bulb is burnt out, something he'd discovered upon going to bed. He must get out of bed and cross the room and turn on a desk lamp if he's to bring the din of the radio to an end.

Even after the radio is silenced, Richard lies in bed awake, his heart still beating fast. Now he worries that this interruption of his sleep may affect his presentation later in the day, and his worries make it hard for him to fall back asleep. Soon he can hear the hotel's housekeeping staff outside his door, in the corridor, pushing their carts and knocking on other doors and chattering among themselves.

Too bad Richard didn't choose to stay at the nearby Perbo Smedley Falls Hotel, one of the chain of hotels founded by Sue Perbo. Sue understands the difference between customer service and customer focus. Beyond training her staff to deliver the friendliest, speediest, most helpful service possible, she also trains them to verify that alarm clocks in vacated rooms have been switched off, that all light bulbs are tested and replaced if necessary, that tissue dispensers are well stocked, that the TV set is working properly and its remote control does not require new batteries, and so on.

Sue is customer focused. She knows that to the guest, a pleasant overall experience is what counts and that the total experience goes far beyond the points of direct contact with staff members.

She knows that if the guest, in the solitary privacy of his or her room, switches on a lamp and the bulb works, the guest won't chalk this up as something remarkable. The bulb is *expected* to work; when it does, the guest doesn't feel a sudden compulsion to call someone at the front desk and thank them for this wonderful service. Sue knows if an unwanted alarm *doesn't* waken the guest prematurely, the well-rested guest won't attribute the uninterrupted night's sleep to good service—it too is simply expected, and the question of service just doesn't enter into it. And yet, Sue understands that someone has to care enough, someone has to be customer focused enough, to verify that certain things are consistently being done behind the scenes to ensure that all these customer expectations will in fact be met during the guest's stay. Sue knows that when these expectations *aren't* met, the total experience suffers, even when the service during actual contact points is quite pleasant on its own.

Only customer-focused businesses can consistently meet or exceed *all* their customers' expectations. Indeed, only the customer-focused businesses even know what their customers' expectations *are*. They know because they're always asking. If the desk clerk handling Richard's checkout procedure were simply to ask him if his stay had been a pleasant one, it might occur to him to mention the incident with the clock radio. Then, if the desk clerk had been made by her employer to appreciate the power and importance of customer focus, it might occur to her to recommend to her manager that the housekeeping staff be instructed to check all clock radio alarms in all vacated rooms. A lot of if's.

In Chapter 12 we'll look at a formal mechanism for asking customers the right kinds of questions to foster greater customer focus. This incessant asking of questions is one of the hallmarks of customer-focused businesses, as illustrated in the following fable.

A TALE OF TWO EATERIES

In a large, fictional city there were once two pizza restaurant chains competing for the same customers. At Chummy Pizza the emphasis was on providing top-notch customer service. The staff at The Pizza Experience concentrated on cultivating a strong customer focus.

Over the years Chummy Pizza earned a reputation for pleasant, cheerful service. Staff members were adept at remembering specific customers' personal preferences and even details about their lives or their families that they could refer to in conversation; this never failed to impress the customers. Regulars began almost to think of the staff at Chummy's as part of their own families. Even if a staffer made a slipup—hot peppers instead of green peppers, say— customers tended to forgive and forget, as one would do with a fond member of the family.

The employees at The Pizza Experience didn't specialize in pleasant chitchat. They were more inclined to ask questions: "What would you like to see us add to our menu?" "How could we make ordering a pizza easier for you?" Armed with the responses from such inquiries, the staff would meet regularly to brainstorm ways to improve the whole experience of being one of their customers.

- When they learned that some customers would like the option of eating pizzas at home, they introduced their city's first pizza take-out service.
- When they later discovered that some customers didn't like going out in bad weather or heavy traffic to pick up pizza, they introduced the city's first pizza delivery service.

- As they opened more and more delivery locations, they realized it was unclear to some customers which location was nearest to their home, and the wrong one would often be called by mistake; this led to longer delivery times and cold pizzas. So they introduced a single, central telephone number to call; staff operators would then forward the order to the appropriate location.

- Some customers lost the printed menus that bore the central number and couldn't be bothered fishing for it in the big telephone directory, so the phone number became a prominent feature in their advertising jingles ("One quick call and you'll be in pizza heaven: five-five-five, fifty-seven, fifty-seven") to help customers memorize it.

- They discovered that quite a few customers tended to call the easily remembered number a second time to find out how much longer the ordered pizza would be, so they introduced their "thirty minutes or it's free" policy.

Nor were all the innovations confined to home-delivery orders:

- The dining room menu offered not only the widest choice of toppings in town but also choices of crust thickness, type of cheese, and type of tomato sauce.

- Rather than ordering from the menu, diners had the option of unlimited slices of fresh pizza from an "all you can eat" Pizza Buffet that offered 10 styles of pizza based on the 10 most popular combinations of toppings.

- The "unlimited free refills of coffee and soft drinks" policy proved to be so popular that similar "unlimited house salad refills" and "unlimited garlic bread" policies were introduced.

- Diners were treated to a different theme every two weeks, with the staff dressed in appropriate costumes and with appropriate music playing over the sound system: Carnival, Beach Party, School Days, Roaring Twenties, Arabian Nights, Harvest Time, Winter Wonderland, Nursery Rhymes, Sunny Italy...the list went on and on.

- If a diner was celebrating a birthday, the entire staff gathered around the table and belted out the rousing Pizza Experience Birthday Song; the honoree was then presented with a complimentary birthday cake topped with lit candles.

- Because lineups tended to form daily at The Pizza Experience, a waiting area called The Side Show was outfitted with comfortable tables and chairs; roving musicians, jugglers, comedians, ventriloquists, balloon manipulators, or magicians kept customers amused while they waited for a table in the dining room. Naturally, coffee and soft drinks were complimentary in the waiting area.

Now it came to pass that both pizza chains had the misfortune of accidentally hiring a less-than-ideal employee.

The bad apple at Chummy Pizza was extremely slow because he felt a frequent need to steal away to the staff washroom for a "smoke break." Most of the pizzas he delivered to tables thus tended to be cold. Cold, too, was his manner with the customers. When one of the faithful regulars would try to strike up a cheerful conversation ("So, what do you think about this weather we've been having lately?") his responses tended to be somewhat curt ("Look, I really don't have time for any of this happy-talk stuff right now; I'm far enough behind as it is.")

His customers were left to eat their cold pizza in cold silence. Chummy Pizza was known for its superb customer service; though customers were prepared to overlook the occasional little slipup, when the service element suddenly disappeared altogether, there wasn't much left to distinguish Chummy's from the competition. A few of the bad apple's unhappy customers complained to management and were absolved of paying their bill. This helped, but they remained leery about returning for fear they'd get stuck with the same server again. Most of the unhappy customers said nothing; they simply left in silence, wondering if maybe it was time to try one of the city's other pizza houses.

Across town, The Pizza Experience had also acquired an extremely slow new employee. What's more, this one never bothered to write orders down and consistently delivered the wrong items. His manner with customers was argumentative and confrontational ("Look, pal, you ordered pepperoni and you *got* pepperoni. Now you want to change you mind, that's fine—but don't go trying to make out like *I'm* the one that screwed up.")

Such lapses in customer service at The Pizza Experience did some damage to customers' perception of the place, no question. Yet there remained so much about the experience that was positive—so many alternate options, so many extras, so many unique and enjoyable aspects unavailable elsewhere—that customers were more inclined to give them another chance. If, for example, they were stuck with the same server on their next visit, they could opt for the Pizza Buffet and bypass him altogether. Furthermore, because the customer-focused staff at The Pizza Experience were always probing for customer feedback, chances are they would learn about a bad apple in their midst in short order and could take appropriate corrective action that much sooner.

The moral of this tale: improving customer *focus* provides a greater strategic and competitive advantage than improving customer service alone.

SETTING THE WOODS ON FIRE

The people who make up a business enterprise collectively expend a certain amount of energy in the daily execution of their tasks and duties. This energy typically gets spread around all over the organization—we can compare it to the heat energy of the sun falling on a meadow on a clear summer day. Some parts of the meadow (those in the shade) may receive a "shade" less warmth than others, but overall the distribution of heat energy is pretty even over a wide area. Now a child comes along with a toy magnifying glass and proceeds to focus some of that heat energy down to a single fine point on the edge of a leaf. Almost at once there is a little wisp of smoke, and then a tiny flame appears, which quickly grows and spreads—and before very long the entire meadow is engulfed in a raging fire. The child, and other creatures living in the meadow, must flee for their own safety. There has been a dramatic and sudden change in the way heat is distributed in the meadow, even though *no new energy was added* to bring about this change. Such is the power of focusing energy.

Energy in most businesses is typically dissipated in all directions; there may be lots of hectic but disjointed activity, sometimes even tugs-of-war pulling in opposite directions and accomplishing little or nothing. The Customer Focus Process outlined at length in Part II represents a method for bringing some of that energy into focus; in this case, the focal point becomes the customer experience. As the consistently successful businesses have discovered, simply focusing the organization's attention on the customer can produce truly dramatic changes—especially when the enthusiasm of both customers and workers begins to spread...like wildfire.

The "better alternative" businesses are increasingly aware that their customers come to them not just for a basic product or service, which they could obtain elsewhere, but for a total experience that *cannot* be duplicated anywhere else.

Such businesses are learning to use the power of the wow factor to gain a competitive advantage over rivals who merely *satisfy* their customers.

For a business to become a Wow Factory over the long term, of course, requires the active participation and involvement of every employee. But how do we make this happen when our employees don't seem particularly motivated to get involved in such initiatives? That's the subject matter of Chapter 3.

Snappy Summary

- ▶ From the customer's point of view we're actually selling the *whole experience* of doing business with us.

- ▶ Increasingly, suppliers are chosen on the basis of how they *add value* to their products and services.

- ▶ The customer expects us to strive very hard to make him or her happy every step of the way.

- ▶ Merely "meeting" customer expectations won't be enough to give us a competitive edge, since our competitors will all be doing the same thing merely to stay in business; the customer experience must include a "wow factor" which *exceeds* expectations.

- ▶ "Customer Service" refers to the quality of the treatment customers receive during *points of contact* with the supplier; "Customer Focus" takes into consideration the quality of the *total customer experience*.

- ▶ Improving customer focus provides a greater strategic and competitive advantage than improving customer service alone.

Chapter Three

Why Are Employees Demotivated?

HOW TO TEACH WORKERS NOT TO GIVE A DAMN

"In times of crisis," an executive once told me, "most businesses tend to bring all their covered wagons into a big circle, and then start shooting *inward*."

It's a familiar enough situation: in bigger organizations, entire divisions at war with each other, whole departments in conflict, employees at all levels not getting along. In smaller businesses, all kinds of petty jealousies and resentments leading to all kinds of discord. Strife, friction, stress—not a recipe for wow factor customer attention.

Where's all this internal tension coming from? There are clues all around if we care to look for them. For example, there's a certain cartoon decorating the walls of offices, factories, and back rooms in just about every workplace in North America. It depicts four little men rolling on the floor with laughter; the caption reads, "You Want It When?" This "humorous" little artifact is everywhere! What is its "harmless" message? It's saying, "You, my colleague, who depend on me for (something) in order to get your own job done, let me advise you that as far as I'm concerned, your needs are a joke. Your requirements make me laugh out loud. In fact, probably the best thing you could do is just turn around and walk out of here and not come back."

There are plenty of variations on the message: Dirty Harry shoving the barrel of his gun in our face with the words, "Go ahead, make my day; tell me it's a rush." Or, from the other side of the counter, "Of course I want it today; if I wanted it tomorrow, I'd ask for it tomorrow." With these and dozens of other similar notices we "jokingly" proclaim that we really have no intention of taking each other's needs seriously. The joke, however, begins to ring a little hollow when the living reality for most employees becomes the daily frustration of dealing with precisely the same mentality depicted so "comically" in the slogans and placards.

Most employees, when they're first hired, genuinely want to do a good job. They soon discover, however, that to do so they must rely on others within the organization for information, or materials, or *something*—and that the something is almost always late, or incomplete, or wrong...or in many cases simply fails to show up altogether. They find themselves going home every night with stomachs tied in knots; they spend their evenings yelling at the spouse and kicking the dog. Eventually they come to the sad realization that it just doesn't pay to care about doing a good job; the more they care, the more frustrated and upset they become. To keep their personal stress levels within manageable limits, they *train* themselves to stop caring. They discover it's a whole lot easier on the nerves to just show up and put in time, to patiently await the next coffee break, the next weekend, the next vacation. They become experts at playing what one manager described to me as "hide-and-seek-for-a-thousand-a-week." In my line of work, which takes me into businesses and organizations of all types and sizes, it is truly heartbreaking to encounter, nearly everywhere I go, armies of perfectly capable workers who have simply stopped caring and have cut themselves off emotionally from their work. Is it really a wonder that our nation is struggling to remain competitive in the global marketplace? The time has come to change the way we think—in this case, the way we think about our colleagues and employees. They are *customers*. They have requirements and expectations, just like external customers; and when we consistently fail to satisfy their needs, they abandon us, just like external customers do. We then incur the hefty costs associated with high turnover; we have to recruit, hire, and train their replacements. (Or, if they've become too demotivated to even bother searching for a better alternative employer, they simply quit *emotionally* but remain on the payroll anyway, to become very expensive noncontributors and nonproducers. We may wake up one morning to discover that they've transformed our whole business into a big charitable nonprofit organization.) We need to apply the principles of customer focus to our internal customers. We have to upgrade the total experience for every employee. It is *we* who have to become perceived as the better alternative employer. We have to make our workers proud and happy to be with us and make workers elsewhere want to join our team. So where do we begin?

WHAT MAKES BOWLING FUN?

In bowling, the object is to knock pins down with a heavy rolling ball. Why would anybody willingly devote time (and pay good money) to pursue such a pointless activity?

Question: When you bowl, are you trying to knock down every pin every time?

Bowler: Yes.

Question: Do you ever succeed?

Bowler: I never have.

Question: Before a game, do you sometimes believe you will succeed in knocking down every pin every time?

Bowler: No. It's just about impossible, really.

Question: But you still *try* to do it.

Bowler: Yes.

Question: Even though you know you won't succeed.

Bowler: Right.

Question: So where does the fun part come in?

Bowler: The more pins I knock down, the more fun I'm having.

Question: Ah, so you're saying the closer you get to this impossible goal of yours, the better you feel.

Bowler: Right.

Question: Even though you know you'll never actually reach the goal itself.

Bowler: Right.

Question: So what do you do when you fail to knock down every pin?

Bowler: I try to analyze what I did wrong and what I could do better. I try new techniques, to see if I can knock down more pins next time.

Question: And when your new technique fails?

Bowler: I try *another* new technique.

Question: And when your new technique succeeds?

Bowler: I'm thrilled. That's why I love this game. And I keep getting better. You should have seen my scores last year compared to now. That's what makes it so much fun.

The bowler might not be aware of it, but he or she is practicing classic quality improvement. Set a challenging goal (zero defects, total customer delight), analyze what's preventing the goal from being reached, and try new approaches to bring the unattainable goal a little closer to reality.

Question: What's the object of *your* game?

Golfer: See that little flag way off in the distance over there? There's a little hole in the ground right there. I'm going to try to send this little white ball flying in that direction by whacking it hard with this club and try to sink it in the little hole.

Question: And this, I gather, is fun?

Golfer: It's a great game. All the fresh air, the walking—I just love it.

Question: Since the walking is so enjoyable, why not just walk over to the little hole and drop the ball in?

Golfer: Well, no, what would be the point of that? No, the rules say you have to hit the ball with one of these clubs.

Question: How many times do you have to hit it?

Golfer: No, see, that's not it. It's not a matter of having to hit it a certain number of times—in fact, you want to hit it as *few* times as possible. Getting the ball in by hitting it just *once* is actually the best. That's ideal.

Question: If you just walked over and dropped it in, you wouldn't even have to hit it that one time.

Golfer: Well, yes, I know, but what would that accomplish? See, that's the whole point of the rules.

Question: And you, sir, the object of your game?

Pool Player: Use this long stick to hit that ball and get it rolling so it will hit each of the other balls and get them rolling into those pockets.

Question: This is fun, presumably?

Pool Player: When it works, yes.

Question: And yours?

Darts Player: Hit the bull's eye in the center of that board with these darts.

Question: Do you manage to hit it very often?

Darts Player: Not too often.

Question: Wouldn't the game be much easier if they just made the bull's eye a whole lot bigger?

Darts Player: I suppose, but then there wouldn't be much point in playing, would there?

Question: And the object of your game, sir?

Pinball Player: Score enough points to win a free game so I can play again and win more free games so I can keep playing for free and winning more games.

In all of these and countless other recreational pursuits, the same pattern: the challenging goal, the striving to get as close to the goal as possible, and the deep satisfaction that results whenever success brings the goal even a little bit closer. These are precisely the kinds of seemingly pointless activities our demotivated, nonproducing employees sit around daydreaming about as they idle away their dreary workshifts ("I'd give anything to be out shooting a few holes of golf today, instead of stuck in this place"). It's the way most workers' entire waking lives are structured—half of it consumed by a boring job, the remainder given over to as much fun stuff away from the job as circumstances and bank account permit.

But what makes selling clothes, or cooking hamburgers, or typing memos seem so boring, while knocking down the same pins over and over again or sending little balls rolling into holes in the ground or along the sides of tables seem so enjoyable? What is it about our jobs, what is it about working for a living that seems to drive all the fun out of the enterprise? This is a big question because it gets at the root of employee demotivation, which is probably the biggest obstacle to the creation of happy customers and, therefore, to the success of our business.

Scenario 1: Welcome, new employees. This is our
primary circuit-breaking facility, and this
is where you'll be working. Your job will
be to use these impact spheres to knock
over those free-standing circuit breakers
at the opposite end of the generator
channel. Regular interruptions of the
circuits is necessary to avoid any
dangerous buildup of voltage levels. Once
you've knocked them down, a resetting
machine will quickly reposition them to
restore the circuit, but that's fine, pay no
attention, just go ahead and knock them
down again. That's basically your job—
you knock them down, the machine will
stand them up again, you knock them
down again. Just keep knocking them
down over and over again until the end
of your shift; then your replacement will
take over. Each shift will last 8 hours;
lunch breaks are 30 minutes. Any
questions?

Please give Scenario 1 a rating on the Boring Job Scale,
from 1 (extremely boring) to 10 (not at all boring).

Scenario 2: The more circuit breaker impacts that take
place per hour, the lower the voltage
buildups and, therefore, the higher our
performance. For this reason we want to
encourage you to try to knock down as
many breakers as possible with each
impact sphere. When all the breakers fall
from a single impact—what we call a
Single Total Random Impact Knockdown
Episode, or STRIKE—you receive a strike

token. These tokens can be redeemed for cash or for time off with pay at the end of each month. Also, the work team that generates the most tokens will win a quarterly championship trophy, along with a range of special prizes. Any questions?

Does Scenario 2 sit any higher on the Boring Job Scale? Knocking pins over or sinking balls in holes or sticking darts in a board or tossing playing cards onto a table or moving pieces around on a checkered board—these do not in themselves make our recreational pursuits enjoyable. The key element is the irresistible appeal of a challenge: "Bet you can't hit that can with this rock." "Race you to the store." "Bet you can't knock every pin down with this ball." It is *the triumph of accomplishing the difficult.*

Watch children at play. As soon as a challenge is met, the rules are changed to make the objective more demanding: "Bet you can't hit it from *this* far back." "Let's see you do that with one hand." "Now do it faster."

The structure imposed by formal rules and a scoring scheme can turn even the most otherwise inane activity into an engrossing game. The challenge then lies in scoring as many *points* as possible, in competing with the point scores of others, or with your own best previous score. The enjoyment derives from having a clear picture of what a perfect performance would look like (a perfect score), having a continuous and immediate means of measuring present performance levels (the current score), and striving to reduce the gap between the current score and a perfect score as the game unfolds. Some of life's most profoundly satisfying and rewarding moments are simply the result of seeing this gap grow narrower. But how does all of this apply to business?

SCORING POINTS WITH CUSTOMERS

It's no coincidence that the leaders in service and quality are always soliciting feedback from their customers. Using methods ranging from simple "How Are We Doing?" cards to elaborate formal surveys, interviews, and focus groups, these businesses give their customers ample opportunity to rate their performance. The ratings become their *scorecard*. They know what a perfect score would look like (every customer delighted every time), the customer feedback gives them a measure of their present performance, and the satisfaction they derive from seeing the gap grow narrower motivates them to strive even harder to become even better.

The key to employee motivation revolves around *making work feel like play*. The rules of the game are simple: you score points every time you meet a customer's expectations. You score extra points when you *exceed* expectations. You lose points when customers are disappointed or frustrated. You lose *extra* points when competitors steal your customers away. You use a measurement system to keep score. The business with the highest score is the winner. Simple. (The chapters in Part II will describe game strategies in more detail.)

Play, by definition, is fun. Work, for most people, is by definition dull and dreary. Yet walk through the door of any business that's winning the customer-pleasing game—the employees don't appear listless or bored or demotivated. On the contrary, they seem energized, enthusiastic, full of boisterous spirits and laughter and camaraderie. They treat their work like play. What do the leaders in these businesses do to help make the workers' jobs feel like play?

CHEERING THE PLAYERS ON

Consider the word *play*. Everyone engages in play activity of one sort or another; some even get paid for it. In the sports stadium, professional athletes play baseball, hockey, or whatever sport they've chosen. Professional musicians, too, play music for a living. Stage actors get paid to play a role in a play.

Consider the word *cheer*. Wherever there are groups of people playing, there are probably onlookers cheering the players on. To cheer is to encourage, to acknowledge, to give the players a feeling of good cheer. So important is the effect of cheering that in some cases certain onlookers are designated cheerleaders; their role is to inspire a greater collective cheering effort.

Playing and cheering go together, by necessity. In sports, not just when points are scored does cheering erupt from the stands; every play elicits cheers. The athletes *require* this constant encouragement from their loyal fans—without it, the quality of their effort would certainly suffer. Similarly, if the traditional applause and ovations were to disappear from the conclusions of performances in concert halls and theaters, to be replaced simply by the quiet, orderly exit of the audience, it would be difficult for musicians and actors to sustain their motivation for very long. Bowlers thrive on the encouraging cheers of their teammates or companions; golfers relish the verbal and physical pats on the back that acknowledge a good score. Even in the informal play settings of the schoolyard and the family rec room, it's common for the players to cheer themselves and each other on. Children do it instinctively. Play just somehow doesn't *feel* like play without cheering to accompany it.

Think of a business you know of, preferably right in your own neighborhood, that excels at delighting customers. Try to arrange a site visit, if possible. As you tour the facilities, you'll probably see evidence of cheering on all sides: photos of employees and teams posted on bulletin boards, highlighting service achievements; letters from delighted customers on proud display; awards, citations, ribbons, trophies, certificates, plaques, news clippings, sales results, productivity charts, all touting the accomplishments of teams and individuals.

If the employees in such businesses tend to behave like players on a winning team, one of the main reasons may be that their management ensures they're *treated* like winners, that they're made to *feel* like winners. If they seem to treat their work like play, it may be because all this cheering and encouragement makes it *feel* like play. They may not need to be part of a bowling league to get their kicks, to feel like they're good at something—they're getting their kicks right from their jobs. Note, too, on your tour of the premises, the conspicuous absence of punch clocks, of posted rules and regulations forbidding this and that, and of other manifestations of prisonlike regimentation. These employees are made to feel like *champions*, not like children or criminals. Management trusts them, gives them the benefit of the doubt, and it shows. Ask these managers if they ever get ripped off, if some employees occasionally take advantage of their liberties. You'll probably be told that it does happen from time to time, but too rarely to outweigh the huge benefits— and profits—that this kind of treatment of employees (that is, internal customers) produces in the long run.

Contrast all of this with the kind of treatment workers receive in *most* businesses—perhaps even in your own.

RULING THE INMATES WITH AN IRON HAND

In the 1967 movie *Cool Hand Luke*, the prison camp bosses are determined to break the spirit of renegade prisoner Luke, played by Paul Newman. They've worked out an effective system for achieving this objective. Boss A first instructs Luke to dig a big, deep hole in the ground. Some hours later Boss B wanders along, expresses horror at the big hole Luke has dug, and angrily commands him to fill it in at once. As soon as the hole is filled, Boss A returns and angrily demands to know why the hole he asked for still isn't dug; he orders Luke to dig it at once. Boss B shows up hours later and expresses outrage that the ugly hole still isn't filled in. And so on—Luke continues digging the hole anew and filling it back in as instructed by his increasingly angry and abusive bosses. Finally, physically exhausted and emotionally drained, he collapses into a weeping, trembling heap at his bosses' feet, begging for their mercy. They know they have him at last. I wonder how many members of the audience watching this scene back in 1967 found themselves able to identify with Luke's ordeal. I wonder how many saw it as an only slightly exaggerated depiction of what they themselves sometimes feel they're going through back on the job, where they work. I wonder how many of their *children* might still be able to make a connection between the scene and their own present-day jobs?

For many workers, making a living still entails spending day after day engaged in tedious, seemingly pointless activities for bosses who are seemingly never satisfied and who frequently issue seemingly contradictory commands. The primary role of the workers' "superiors" is to constantly point out to the "subordinates" (or should they be called "inferiors"?) what it is they're doing wrong.

The workplace is like a prison; the superiors are law enforcement watchdogs, ensuring that the inferiors adhere to all rules and regulations at all times. The workers are constantly being corrected and directly or indirectly reprimanded. They spend the bulk of their time dealing with crises, putting out fires, scrambling to recover from fumbles and errors. Customers are usually angry, frustrated, even hostile. The workers cannot help but conclude that they're working for a loser of a business, which makes them personally feel like losers just for being a part of it. They're embarrassed to admit to friends and relatives that they work for an outfit held in such low regard by both its external customers and its employees (or internal customers).

And now we're going to come along and exhort them to start behaving like winners? Well, good luck.

Before we can expect them to start showing us how they're going to change their ways, we need to show them how we're prepared to change *ours*. We have to remove our cop hats, stop worrying about enforcing laws and rules, and put on our coach hats, start worrying about cheering the players on, celebrating their little successes, and making them feel like winners. We've got to make working in this place more *fun*.

Snappy Summary

- ▶ Colleagues and employees are customers; when we consistently fail to satisfy their needs, they abandon us, just like external customers do.

- ▶ Customer-focused businesses treat their workers like champions, not like children or criminals.

- ▶ Most so-called play activities comprise a challenging goal, an effort to get as close to the goal as possible, and the deep satisfaction that results whenever success brings the goal even a little bit closer.

- ▶ The key to employee motivation revolves around making work feel like play.

▶ The rules for playing the customer focus game: you score points every time you meet or exceed a customer's expectations; you lose points when customers are disappointed or when competitors steal your customers away; the business with the most points is the winner.

Chapter Four

How Do I Set the Stage for Success?

IMPORTANT FIRST STEP: DO NOT HIRE A CONSULTANT

For most businesses, once the decision is made to get serious about improving the customer experience, it's not too difficult to pinpoint the primary trouble spots that require immediate attention. The problems that customers complain about most loudly and most often usually need to be addressed first.

Studies conducted by such research organizations as the Washington, D.C.-based Technical Assistance Research Program (TARP) indicate that only about 1 in every 25 unhappy customers will actually complain; the rest simply take their business elsewhere. It means we've found another opportunity to change the way we think—in this case, about complaining customers—in order to make our businesses more successful.

When an unhappy customer goes to the trouble of asking to speak to someone for the purpose of lodging a complaint, he or she is voluntarily coming forward to share some very valuable information with us. It's as if he or she were saying, "I know something you don't know. I know there's something you're doing that's ticking me off (and therefore probably also ticking off 25 other people who can't be bothered to tell you about it). I'm prepared to tell you about it; in fact,

I may even have some recommendations to make regarding how the situation can be improved. And best of all, I'm prepared to give you all this useful data *completely free of charge*." So how do most businesses respond to this offer? Usually with something along the lines of, "Get out of here you sniveling, whining pest, and don't come back." We can hire high-priced consultants to advise us where and how to improve, or we can let our customers give us the very same information for free.

A customer with a complaint should be treated like *royalty*. Not only do we want to hear your complaint, sir or madam, but please sit down and make yourself comfortable while I round up some other people who should also be here to hear this; and could we impose upon you to approach us the next time you're in to let us know if we've corrected the situation to your satisfaction?

The *way* we listen to complaints is critical. Above all else, under no circumstances, ever, should we dispute the customer's account of what happened, even if we know for certain there are glaring inaccuracies in his or her report. *We are not there to defend ourselves*—we are there to *learn*. Statements such as "The reason that happened is we were short staffed at the time" or "From what I hear, our competitors are even worse than we are in this regard" or "It was our supplier's mistake; you can't blame us for things outside of our control" simply make it clear to complaining customers that they're wasting their time, that we're far more interested in getting off the hook than in finding ways to permanently improve the way we do things. The emphasis should be on encouraging the customer to get everything off his or her chest; there'll be plenty of time to discuss and debate the details later, outside of the customer's earshot.

Once businesses begin to appreciate how valuable their customers' feedback can be, they usually begin to solicit more of it. Not content to hear from the 1 out of 25 unhappy customers who complains, they give *all* their customers ample opportunities to rate their performance. These ratings become the scorecard by which they assess how well (or poorly) they're playing the customer focus game. Such data are invaluable—yet there's a simple way to make customer feedback even *more* useful.

The traditional approach limits the request for feedback to a performance rating: how well did we do in terms of food preparation, or cleanliness, or friendliness, on a scale from abysmal to superb, or some variation thereupon. This is basically a report card. It gives us nice, easy-to-quantify data that simplifies calculating averages and plotting trends. But our customers may have additional useful information to share, if we know how to ask for it. Some ratings cards allow space at the bottom for comments or suggestions; this is getting warmer, but it's still too vague, too broad, too "blue sky." As we'll discover in Part II, the real key in unlocking creative ideas and innovative approaches lies in asking the right questions in the right way.

For example, instead of just asking our customers "How well did we do," we should also be asking them things like, "What could we be doing differently that would make things more convenient or pleasant for you?" Or, "What are some of the frustrations you'd like to see us eliminate from our interactions with you?" Or, "What's something we could do that would be totally unexpected and would make doing business with us a much more delightful experience for you?" You get the idea. We want the question(s) to intrigue the customer: "Hmmmm, that's an interesting question, let me think about that for a second." No consultant on earth, not even the best and highest paid of the bunch—indeed, not even the all-knowing author of this book—will ever be able to provide you with better ideas for delighting your customers than the ideas you'll get for free from your customers themselves. If you can inspire even a few of them to spend a few moments thinking on your behalf about things you could be doing to gain a competitive advantage, you've hired them as free consultants; in all the world, they're the most knowledgeable experts on what it would take to delight your particular customers. (Would payment in the form of a complimentary lunch or a handful of discount coupons be too exorbitant a fee for expertise of this calibre?)

The trick lies in knowing what to ask and how to ask it. The chapters in Part II will spell out in fine detail what to ask your *internal* customers (employees and colleagues) in order to generate innovative improvement ideas; please bear in mind as you review them that many of these same questions can also be asked of the external customer, as we'll discuss in more detail when we look at focus groups in Chapter 12.

IMPORTANT SECOND STEP: WASTE NO MONEY ON ADVERTISING

Here's an eye-opening little experiment I encourage you to try. Part One: pretend, just for the fun of it, that the very next *new* customer that calls or walks into your place of business is actually on a secret mission. Unknown to your workers, a group of 16 people is considering selecting your business as a supplier over your prime competitor; they've enlisted the person that just called or walked in to check you out on their behalf. Depending on how the mystery shopper ends up feeling about the treatment he or she receives, your firm will or won't get the ongoing business of all 16 customers. Now, just for fun, and without saying a word to your employees, go into the workplace and actually watch the transaction with the next new customer unfold. Remember, although this customer may appear perfectly nonchalant, he or she is actually observing everything with a super critical eye. Cleanliness, friendliness, helpfulness—everything is being rated. At the conclusion of the transaction, do an assessment of your own: what is the percentage of likelihood that on the basis of the mystery shopper's experience you'll get the business of the 16 customers?

Part Two: imagine, now, that 1 of the group of 16 decides to tip you off ahead of time to give you a better chance. Imagine that you're able to alert your staff to watch for a certain individual in certain attire due to arrive at a certain time. Every employee now understands that this shopper represents the potential business of 16 customers; whatever amount he or she spends can be multiplied by 16 to get a true sense of his or her worth to the business—and this total can be further multiplied by the number of transactions the group is likely to conduct over time. Armed with this awareness, are your employees likely to treat the customer any differently? Will you be more likely to get the business of the 16? By how much will your percentage of likelihood increase?

Well now, pay close attention. I've got some important news for you. Your next new customer *does* represent 16 other potential customers. I'm not kidding.

Research from the aforementioned TARP organization indicates that unhappy customers typically share their horror stories with 10 other people. Satisfied customers, the research shows, are inclined to tell five others about their happy experience. This means that making a single customer unhappy can result in the loss of a total of sixteen customers: the original unhappy customer, plus 10 more who after hearing a horror story decide to stay away, plus an additional 5 who might have decided to come aboard if they'd heard a happy story, but didn't, and so don't. (We lose this last bunch without ever meeting them; we haven't even had a chance to *irritate* them and they're gone!) Every unhappy customer is the unofficial representative of 15 others. Naturally, these numbers represent averages—if we *really* upset a customer, many more than 10 may hear about it. (If somebody really upsets yours truly, I get to tell *10,000* people about it!) Customers who are profoundly delighted will likewise be inclined to share their experience with a greater number of people.

Everyone knows that positive word of mouth is the most effective form of advertising in the world. We spoke earlier about hiring customers as consultants; let's go one better. Let's also put them to work for us as *goodwill ambassadors*. Instead of pouring money into advertising designed to tell everyone how wonderful we are, let's get our customers doing the telling for us—for free. Let's redirect our advertising money toward giving employees the training and the incentives they need to blow customers' socks off with a level of attention and care that exceeds all expectations. Then let's sit back and let our dazzled customers spread the good word on our behalf.

There'll still be a need for advertising that advises customers of special price reductions, sales, promotions, and so on—basically paid news releases, designed more to inform than to persuade. But advertising designed to convince customers that we're a better alternative to the competition may turn out to be a big waste of money. Let's start putting that money to better use. If we *become* the better alternative, our delighted customers will voluntarily take on the task of convincing others that it's so.

TIME ISN'T MONEY ANYMORE

In the past, attitudes about the value of time were considerably more relaxed than is the case today. With industrialization and a growing emphasis on productivity and efficiency came the need to promote a general awareness that wasting *time* was the equivalent of wasting *money*; the notion that "time is money" was born.

Times have changed since the early days of the industrial era. Has our attitude about time kept pace with the changing times?

Time is *not* the equivalent of money. Money is a renewable resource. It can be lost and then regained. It can be hoarded in quantity and held in reserve. Money can even be used to generate more money. Time, however, is a finite, nonrenewable resource. It passes through our fingers at a fixed rate over which we have absolutely no control. It cannot be held in reserve. And when our personal allocation runs out, as eventually it must, there's simply no more to be had. Time is much more precious than money.

And therein lies an opportunity to siphon some business away from the competition.

FASTER IS BETTER

One hour photofinishing. Delivery by next day anywhere in the USA. Pizza in 30 minutes or it's free. Your new glasses ready in an hour. In by 9, out by 5. Speedy turnaround. Same day service. No waiting. Instant results.

Buy from us, more and more businesses are declaring, and we'll save you time as well as—or even instead of—money. Everything else being equal, the business that does business more quickly will do more business.

The next time you find yourself trapped in a line, in a bank or a supermarket or a movie theater or the place where you get your driver's license updated (that is, at any business that hasn't quite caught on to the power of customer focus yet), observe very carefully what happens when another wicket is opened or another lane put into service. Watch how customers who had been standing quietly, passively, almost as if half asleep, are suddenly furiously scrambling for a favorable position at the head of the new line. What you're seeing is a reenactment, in miniature, of how customers in general react when presented with a better alternative (or, more specifically in this case, a *quicker* alternative).

One almost sure-fire way to help your customers think of your business as the better alternative is to make it the quicker alternative. The following chapter explores some of the dangers associated with careless cost cutting; for now, let's just say that as a rule of thumb, a focus on *time* cutting will probably do more to help the bottom line than will a focus on cost cutting. The Customer Focus Process outlined in Part II will help you identify opportunities to delight your customers at every stage of the customer experience; in general terms, taking up less of the customer's time is an almost foolproof way to produce delight. Businesses with a strong customer focus are constantly asking, "What could we do to speed up this part of the process?" "How could we shorten the delay at this point?" "How could this be simplified so it wouldn't take as long?"

It frequently turns out that the only reason we do things a certain way is that we've *always* done them that way. When the way we do things creates needless extra steps in a process, or produces unnecessary complications and delays, or leads to more opportunities for error, we need to be prepared to challenge our standard, traditional approaches. Having always done things a certain way is *not* the best reason to go on doing them the same way. We must cultivate our ability to sniff out opportunities to speed things up, to keep things moving along, to become the quicker alternative.

TAKING THE LEAD

The issue of leadership is a popular topic these days. In the political sphere, as in the business world, people are *hungry* for strong leadership. They're praying for someone who can, and will, lead them into a less stressful, more secure future.

In the absence of effective leadership, any attempt to introduce change—even such desirable change as a transition from dreary todays to better tomorrows—tends to quickly degenerate into anarchy and confusion. With no one there to keep pointing the way, people soon lose their bearings; they start moving in different directions and wind up scattered farther apart than before. The effort to make things better frequently succeeds only in making things worse.

The role of the leader, at the most fundamental level, is to *inspire others to follow*. This is not an administrative or technological issue—it's a human issue. It bypasses that anonymous, faceless entity known as "the workforce" and taps directly into the very hearts and minds of individual persons.

Alas, holding a leadership *position* in a business does not automatically confer leadership *ability* upon the holder. Nor, alas, is leadership the same thing as management. An effective manager might skillfully run the day-to-day operations of the business for as long as things remain constant and stable and still be utterly incapable of enlisting worker support for an effort to change the way the business operates when such a change becomes necessary. All leaders have a choice. They can attempt to rule by force, or they can attempt to inspire voluntary followership— leadership by intimidation versus leadership by inspiration.

The first option always seems the quickest and easiest; lazy and impatient leaders always favor it. In so doing, they're ignoring the many blood-soaked lessons of history. Leadership by intimidation *never* succeeds in the long run. The enslaved and oppressed produce as little as they can get away with, while their minds and energies remain focused only on finding a way to put an end to their oppression. Any opportunity for sabotage and, ultimately, for liberation will be seized.

The second option takes longer to produce results. People won't voluntarily change their beliefs or behaviors unless they're consistently presented with compelling incentives for doing so. But once people finally make up their minds, once their imaginations are fired up and their sense of purpose ignited, they can blaze a scorching path across the pages of history. The great triumphs of the ages have all been the product of simple people inspired by visionary leaders to achieve heroic objectives. Today many of these leaders, in politics, in business, in science and the arts, are revered as demi gods. And yet was—and is—their approach so godlike?

The secrets of effective leadership are not all that secret, nor even particularly difficult to put into practice, for that matter. Yet their skillful application remains a rarity. Why? Because, for most leaders, doing so would entail changing the way *they* do some things. And while they may find their workers' resistance to change galling and infuriating, their own resistance to change is at least as great. Leadership involves influencing the way others think in order to influence their behavior. The simple truth is that to master these skills, it will first be necessary to change the way we ourselves think and behave.

So how do we begin thinking and behaving like a leader? How do we go about inspiring our troops to follow our lead toward a new way of doing business? The question has a four-part answer.

LEADERSHIP SECRET 1: THE MISSION

If you're standing still, how am I supposed to follow you? You need to be going someplace. In other words, you need to be considering the introduction of some sort of change in the way your business does business. Your *mission* describes what the change is going to be and how you intend to make the change happen.

Hope to increase your market share by 20 percent in the next two years? Planning to accomplish this by increasing your workers' sense of teamwork and customer focus? Figuring on introducing some in-house training to get your employees moving in that direction? That's a mission. Is it time to diversify your product line? Open another operation across town or across the world? Increase productivity by 30 percent without adding new staff?

Your mission is your strategy statement; it answers the question, "What's our current business objective?" It describes the destination to which you intend to *lead* your business. Clearly, it's pretty difficult to lead if there's no place to lead to. Many businesses are hurting today precisely because their leadership is frantically engaged in an all-consuming effort to stay put and go nowhere, a strategy that inspires workers to similarly generate a lot of commotion that changes nothing. A business with no specific mission beyond continued existence, one day at a time, is a business without many days of existence left.

The mission needs to be sufficiently challenging to capture the imaginations of the employees yet not be *so* difficult that it seems unattainable. The right balance is struck when employees collectively feel, "We can do it. It won't be easy, but we can do it." Ideally, the mission should embody an objective that unifies all the employees against a common enemy—the competition. Let's stop clobbering each other, the mission should suggest, and start clobbering *them*.

Is your business driven by a mission? If not, it means everyone's energies are focused on accomplishing nothing in particular—and that's almost certainly what *will* be accomplished over the long term. The simple development of a mission affords you a golden opportunity to introduce a powerful leadership component into your management style. I'll leave the fine details of your mission up to you; in general terms I'd just like to point out that the creation of happy customers provides an ideal framework for the development of a strategy to siphon customers (and profits) away from the competition.

LEADERSHIP SECRET 2: THE VISION

Okay, so you're headed someplace, and you'd like me to follow you there. Truth is, I'm not so convinced the place you have in mind is really going to be any better for me personally than the place I am in now—you'll have to get me a little more excited before I'll be ready to start moving in any radical new directions.

Every true leader begins with a mission; great leaders *communicate* their mission in a very special way. They paint a compelling picture of what achieving the mission will *look* like. The vision answers the question "How will we know when we've accomplished the mission?" It describes what we'll *see* that will tell us it's time to celebrate our success.

Photojournalists train themselves to think in terms of capturing the decisive moment. What single visual image, they ask themselves, will sum up the whole story on the front page or cover? Our recollection of the major events in recent history often revolves around such images. Refugees crowding aboard American helicopters from rooftops in Saigon. Crowds celebrating atop a crumbling Berlin Wall. A lone student defying tanks in Tiennamen Square. A footprint on the moon.

JFK's mission may have been to regain supremacy in aerospace technology over the Russians after their groundbreaking Sputnik launch—a very worthwhile objective, though not particularly sexy. His vision, however, was a man on the moon before the end of the decade. This not only required accomplishing the mission, it incorporated an exciting competitive challenge ("Hey, you Russians, bet we can beat you to the moon!") and provided a clear, decisive moment ("One small step for man") that gave half the world the signal to break into cheering and applause.

A less visionary leader might have quietly overseen the advancement of aerospace technology in the labs and back rooms of obscure research facilities across the continent. Though the mission might still have ultimately been accomplished, this approach would have made it difficult to pinpoint a specific date or moment when success was achieved. Today, most people old enough to appreciate what was happening when Neil Armstrong took his small step can vividly remember witnessing the moment on live television.

Walt Disney built an immensely successful business empire on the strength of his personal vision. After his death in 1966, the company he founded began to flounder. By 1984 Disney's corporate earnings had reached such a critical low point that the company was vulnerable to the attacks of corporate raiders. Enter Michael Eisner, another bold visionary—and Disney's earnings skyrocketed from $98 million in 1984 to $824 million in 1990, with no end in sight. Such is the power of effective leadership.

The visionary leader gives people a precious gift—the *opportunity to participate in a triumph*. With triumph comes jubilation and a sense of worth. We tend to look back on such moments of personal and collective triumph as the high points of our lives.

How do you create an inspiring vision for your enterprise? You train yourself to think the way photojournalists think. They relate the news *visually*, in pictures. You want the successful achievement of your vision to feel like news; you have to create in your mind the image of a decisive moment that would represent success, that would give people something to cheer about, and then describe what that image looks like.

For example, consider the vision statement "Our customers become crazy about us." A good objective but not a very compelling vision. How many customers? How crazy? How will we know when it's time to celebrate? Version two: "We win the *Consumer Digest* annual Customers' Choice Award for our region within the next two years." This is better—we now know for sure whether we made it . But how will the news be announced? Where's our decisive moment of triumph, our cue to break into wild applause? Version three: We organize an Academy Awards-type banquet for the employees and families of those businesses that were regional finalists in the competition. We invite representatives from *Consumer Digest,* and from the mayor's office, and the Chamber of Commerce, and the press, to attend. *Here* the winners will be announced. Even if we lose, the banquet serves to recognize that we're among the finalists, the best there is; our determination to win next year will be that much greater. But our vision, of course, is the image of the mayor breaking the evening's suspense by announcing the winner—and handing *us* the award. Now we've got something to cheer about, something to *strive* for. We've got a moment of triumph that can be captured in a photograph, mounted over a desk, and trigger fond memories for years to come.

Incidentally, as far as I know, there's no such thing as the *Consumer Digest* Customers' Choice Award—it's just a made-up example to illustrate a point. When we think about our mission, we need to create a visual element that captures the decisive moment of success; this becomes our vision. If the Academy Awards banquet sounds impossibly ambitious, think on a smaller scale. At the very least, rig up a prominent "thermometer" that graphically displays progress toward the objective or a telethon-style tote board to disclose the changing numbers. And when the goal is reached, start the sirens and ring the bells; abandon your small-scale thinking and make with some big-scale hoopla. Create a moment of triumph to unleash some serious celebratory shenanigans. If you're going to inspire me to follow you, make our destination an exciting, fun place to be.

LEADERSHIP SECRET 3: THE COMMITMENT

Okay, you've painted a fabulous picture of where you want to lead me, but are you really leading me there, or just *leading me on*? I don't want to get my hopes up only to find out it'll never happen because you're not willing to do what's necessary to make it happen. If you're as crazy with determination to succeed as you say you are, then maybe it's about time to get yourself committed.

It's a funny thing about commitment—if your employees aren't convinced yours is real, you can demonstrate genuine commitment a hundred times in a row and they'll still be unconvinced. Yet demonstrate a *lack* of commitment even once and they'll conclude with certainty that your commitment is *not* real. Sooner or later, the leader will be expected to lead, not with inspiring words alone but with inspiring *deeds*. And in this regard, money talks. All across the business landscape, bosses are announcing their latest cost-cutting schemes to their workers. It's a time of belt-tightening, of cutting back on some of the frills, of trimming the budgetary fat. No more lavish staff picnics—we just can't afford them. No more having Santa distribute presents to the workers' kids at the Christmas party—too expensive. Got to cut our long-distance phone charges. Got to cut back on the amount of paper we use. Got to find ways to use fewer paper clips, fewer staples.

This sort of thing has been going on for decades. The message it sends to workers is crystal clear: we, the leadership in this organization, have run all out of ideas for increasing our income, so instead we're shifting our attention to decreasing our outlay. Maybe that'll help, until we can think of something better.

With the onset of fiscal distress, the bean counters come swooping in, vulture-like. The human dynamics of motivation and inspiration are things they frequently know nothing about; but cutting costs—ah, this they understand. Here, at last, is their chance to shine. All this equipment, all this capacity—do we really need this much? Let's sell off a good part of it; that'll produce a hefty chunk of cash right there. It'll also reduce our floor space requirements; the savings in rent charges alone will be stupendous, and that'll go right to the bottom line. We'll finally be out of the red! Plus, wait, there's more good news—with our reduced capacity, we'll no longer need as many employees! All that monstrous overhead suddenly gone—fantastic! We'll be *rolling* in cash!

Of course, by this time, the (remaining) employees understand the situation very well. Theirs is a ship that's going down. They're on the losing team. It's game over. Even if by a miracle the business were to recover, the bad taste would linger for a long time. No one would be prepared to invest quite as much effort or enthusiasm as before.

Is all of this intended to suggest that reducing fiscal waste is a bad thing? Au contraire, improving organizational efficiency means, by definition, eliminating waste. When we bring a leadership component (which is to say, a human component) into our decision-making process, however, it forces us to evaluate any proposed action in terms of how well it does—or doesn't—demonstrate commitment to our vision. Before we start wielding the cost-cutting machete indiscriminately, it forces us to make a vital and clear distinction between *costs* and *investments*.

Businesses with a history of success also as a rule have a history of spending considerable sums on morale builders for their internal customers (i.e., employees): parties, celebrations, promotional items, gifts, and so on. They recognize, too, that the whole morale question does not revolve around their internal customers alone. Creating happy external customers also has costs associated with it, and successful businesses have a history of willingly incurring these costs as well. Seeing this, the less successful businesses might be inclined to mutter, "Yeah, sure, it's easy for *them* to go all out, they can afford it, with their profits." But this misses the whole point entirely.

Successful businesses don't invest in internal/external customer morale because they happen to be profitable; they do it because they know it helps *make* them profitable. The cause-and-effect factors are reversed. Businesses that intend to make their workers feel like winners once they become a little more successful somehow never seem to become quite successful enough to do so. Conversely, those that routinely invest in morale builders for their workers continue doing so even when profits hit a slump—they recognize that it will take the collective effort of a fired-up team of employees to reverse the downturn, and this makes the investment in employee enthusiasm and motivation more important than ever.

Cost cutting that reduces waste is to be encouraged. Cost cutting that cripples our ability to generate revenue can have catastrophic—and even fatal—consequences.

At Dwindletech Industries, the account reps are advised that effective next month, they will have to fly economy class on all business trips; this measure, they are told, will support the new corporate focus on improving profitability. The CEO at Downward Spiral & Associates announces that for the first time in eight years, there won't be a Christmas party for the staff and families; the cost is simply prohibitive, especially in view of the current slump in sales. At Peter Out Automotive Repair, Peter himself decides to discontinue their long-standing tradition of providing complimentary car washes with routine repair work; maybe it's something that can be reinstated once the economy starts picking up. Over at Topples And Burns' Software Mart, the decision is made to shut down the 24-hour Help Hotline. "We're lucky if we get one or two calls a night," explains general manager Dick Topples. "It just doesn't make sense to go on paying a software expert to sit there and do nothing all night long."

Six months after these decisions are made, some intriguing developments come to light. At Dwindletech, overall sales have suddenly dropped to dangerously low levels, the lowest in the firm's history. It seems the account reps hated flying away from home and family on business trips to begin with; now that they're forced to fly economy class, where dinner is a bag of peanuts and half a plastic cup of warm soda, they've simply elected to stop pursuing most out-of-town accounts altogether.

With springtime comes some new business at Downward Spiral; to meet the increased demand, senior management asks the staff if they'd be willing to come in on Saturdays at time-and-a-half for a few weeks. To their amazement, the staff unanimously refuses. As one supervisor puts it, "Why should I break my back for this outfit? They can't even be bothered to give us our Christmas party. Last Christmas my youngest boy was just old enough to attend the party for the first time. His two older brothers were telling him all about it for weeks; he couldn't wait to go. Then, at the last minute, management decides to cancel it, just like that. My little guy was heartbroken. People around here have had enough of this kind of treatment. Now a few new orders start coming in and we're supposed to give up half our weekends for them, just like that? They can forget it, as far as I'm concerned." Management is forced to bring in untrained temporary help to handle the overflow; the additional costs wipe out all the profits, and the error rate soars. Customer problems and complaints begin taking up the regular staff's time during the normal work week, causing overall schedules to begin slipping badly.

Peter Out just can't understand where the customers have gone; even his regulars don't seem to be bringing their cars in for repairs any more. As luck would have it, he bumps into one of his former regulars in the supermarket.

"Eddie," he says, "how come you never bring your car in any more?"

"Well," says Eddie, "to tell you the truth, now that you've stopped doing the car wash thing, I've been bringing my car into National Tailpipe. They're right in my neighborhood."

"Do *they* wash your car?"

"No, but they give free coffee. Plus they're nice and handy. Your place is in a scruffy area halfway across town. The only reason I used to go all the way out there was I thought the car wash thing was pretty neat. Turns out there's a car wash just around the corner from National Tailpipe."

The more former customers Peter runs into, the more he hears that the location of his business is unappealing or inconvenient; the free car wash, he discovers, was the main attraction all along. He discontinued it because he felt he could no longer afford it; now he can afford it even less.

Dick Topples has been doing some similar research to pinpoint why sales at the Software Mart have been falling off so badly. It seems people stopped thinking of the place as the better alternative the moment the 24-hour help hotline was shut down and began shopping around elsewhere. "I don't get it, Floyd," Dick tells one ex-customer. "You never *used* the hotline. Not *once*. What difference did it make if it was shut down?"

"The thing is," Floyd explains, "I knew it was there. It was just a good feeling to know that you cared enough to have somebody sitting there ready to help me if I needed it. It's like when I moved into my condo—the thing that sold me on that building was the beautiful huge indoor pool. I moved in seven years ago. I've never used that pool once. But I *know it's there*. When you shut your hotline down, it was like suddenly you just didn't care as much."

Wealth costs money. We need to constantly be asking ourselves what effect our proposed short-term cost-containment measures will have on our ability to generate wealth in the long term. Our focus needs to shift from reducing our spending to increasing our earnings.

Dwindletech's account reps are the primary generators of wealth for the firm. Do not make their revenue-generating activities less appealing for them by consigning them to the economy section of the plane. Besides keeping them in first class, provide them with complimentary portable CD players! Give them free laptop computers! The more broke you are, the less cash you have on hand, the more important for you to invest in making the earning of new revenue as attractive as possible for those whose job it is to go out there and make it happen. Beg, borrow, or steal the money you need to do it, but one way or another, make those people enjoy creating new wealth for the business *so much* they just can't wait to get at it.

Do not discontinue "frivolous" and "expensive" activities that make employees feel good about the business they work for; you'll be robbing them of their incentive to help the business succeed. Instead, invest every penny you can scrape up in activities designed to motivate them to give their all and to do their best.

Freebies and extras that help external customers see your business as a better alternative do *not* qualify as waste; they're solid business investments. To discontinue them is to drive your customers into the waiting arms of your competitors.

Strategies that revolve solely around reducing costs or bolstering profits typically represent a short-term focus; shifting the emphasis to the creation of happy customers requires a longer-term focus. You must ask yourself: *Am I in business for the short term or for the long term?* Conditioned by our disposable, instant-gratification way of life, we may as an entire society be at risk of losing our ability to plan for the long term. Three years from today may seen like an unimaginably distant time to be planning for—and yet that day will arrive whether we will have planned well for it or not. Businesses can go from prosperous to *bankrupt* in three years. It's something you need to consider very carefully.

Short-term thinking or long-term thinking—workers who are skeptical about your commitment will be watching for an answer to that same question. Do you believe in your vision sufficiently to *invest* in it? Are you prepared to visibly put your money where your mouth is? In the final analysis, this becomes the ultimate demonstration of your commitment to make your vision a reality—and as an employee, unless I see solid proof that your determination to get there is unshakeable, I probably won't see much point in taking this great and noble vision of yours very seriously.

LEADERSHIP SECRET 4: THE EXAMPLE

All right, I'm sold. You're headed to an exciting place, and nothing's going to deter you from getting there. Now you'd like me to follow you. Very well, then, I shall begin by following your *example*.

They arrive unexpectedly, as a rule. Sometimes they happen in rapid succession, sometimes with long intervals between them. They can be quiet and subtle and pass almost unnoticed; or they can create such a stir that they're the only thing people talk about for weeks. They're the insidious little situations you find yourself in every so often, situations where you must choose between one particular course of action or another. These decisions can often seem relatively trivial at the time, and yet they can afterward turn out to have brought your entire leadership credibility crashing down like a house of cards. You may not always realize it at the time, but these situations place you on the hot seat. Once you've declared your commitment to a vision, it's probably only a matter of time before you find yourself in a hot seat-uation.

Example: at a general staff meeting, an employee asks, "If management around here considers us workers so dang-blasted important all of a sudden, how come management gets reserved parking spaces right up near the front door and the rest of us have to scramble for whatever's left over?" Before you bark at the ingrate that he should siddown, shaddup, and be darned thankful he still has a job, note how quiet the room has suddenly become. This is one of the telltale signs that you're in the hot seat—all movement and conversation abruptly stops, all eyes turn to you. You suddenly have to make a decision—one that could make or break the credibility of your commitment to create happy internal and external customers.

Let's freeze the moment before you respond. A variety of thoughts run through your mind: If I give in to this loud-mouth, every other disgruntled employee will try to get in on the act—I'll be making ridiculous concessions till dooms-day. I didn't spend the past 15 years climbing my way up the corporate ladder just to have some two-bit nobody tell me I should start giving up all the privileges I worked so hard to earn.

Thoughts are running through the workers' minds, too: Now we'll find out if this happy internal customers thing is all-talk-no-action. Let's see how our fearless leader wea-sels out of this one. Oh boy, this is gonna be good.

It's all up to you. You're the one asking your workers to inconvenience themselves by voluntarily changing the way they do their work, rather than clinging to the more comfortable, familiar way of doing things. Are you prepared to inconvenience yourself too, and also take on some new ways of doing things? You're asking them to trust you, to have faith that you won't lead them astray or take advantage of them. Are you prepared to trust *them* too, and have faith that *they* won't take excessive advantage of any new freedoms and privileges you may pass their way? Will your leadership style be based on a "do as I say, not as I do" approach? Do you feel the sacrifices others will have to make do not apply to you by simple virtue of the fact that you're the boss? If so, it means that whether you admit it or not, you're ultimately opting for leadership by intimidation rather than for leadership by inspiration.

The loudmouth ingrate is an unhappy customer—one of the few brave enough to come forward with a formal complaint. In voicing his displeasure over the parking arrangement, this worker is probably expressing a sentiment held by other, less outspoken workers as well. You may resent him for his bellyaching, or, if you're prepared to look at it in a different way, you may instead feel grateful to him. He has handed you, on a silver platter, in a totally spontaneous way that could never have been convincingly contrived ahead of time, the means to prove more effectively than words alone ever could the true extent of your commitment.

"The point you raise about the parking arrangement is actually a pretty good one, Raoul. Maybe the thing to do would be to redesignate the management spots as Customer Champion spots. Maybe throughout each month workers could earn little tokens of merit for anything they do that delights customers; at the end of each month, those holding the most tokens would be entitled to use one of the designated parking spots for the entire following month. Maybe the holder of the most tokens would get *my* spot for the month, right at the door. Raoul, would you be willing to give some thought to something along these lines and make some recommendations about the best way to implement such a system? And as for the management team, well, I guess we'll have to start scrambling for parking places just like everybody else has always done." What effect would this type of response have on the other workers? Would the gain in your leadership credibility be worth the loss of your reserved parking spot?

This kind of situation puts you on the hot seat precisely because everyone recognizes it as a clear-cut challenge of your credibility. No amount of eloquent words, no succession of impassioned speeches can ever come close to having the same sort of impact—positive or negative—that your selected course of action will have.

Virtually every instance of a customer (internal or external) lodging a complaint puts you on the hot seat. But, as suggested in the previous chapter, if you're aware of this, you're in a position to actually *welcome* encounters with gripers and grumblers—they're providing you with the best possible answer to your question, "How can I prove that I really mean business?" (Or, "That my commitment remains as strong as ever?") They're providing you with the best possible opportunity to *lead by example*, the single most effective leadership strategy of all.

Customers need not actually complain aloud in order to put you on the hot seat. Anytime you observe any sort of customer dissatisfaction whatsover, you're confronted with an opportunity to lead by example; do *whatever it takes* to transform this unhappy (internal or external) customer into a delighted one. If it requires giving away a freebie or (for an employee) some time off or entails some other reasonable cost, incur the expense without hesitation. Think of it as part of your advertising budget, your investment in positive word of mouth, the most potent form of advertising money can buy. Keep your eyes open for opportunities to demonstrate, again and again, for an audience of one (who'll spread the word, don't worry) or of many, what producing happy customers looks like. Even more important, show your workers what it *feels* like. Make *them* experience delight, as often as possible, so that they know firsthand what sensation it is they're trying to evoke in their own customers.

It is precisely in the way the leader responds to a challenge of credibility, or introduces an unexpected element of delight in simple routine transactions with others, that he or she can touch and move people. The leader's role is to inspire—and an inspiring example inspires best. The great irony (and tragedy) about leadership by example is that every leader is already doing it, even if they've never given it a thought. The moment anyone assumes a leadership position in a business, their actions and behaviors begin to influence the actions and behaviors of others. Those unskilled leaders who mistrust workers inspire the workers to similarly mistrust their customers. Frustrated employees express their frustration in behavior that frustrates customers. Workers that feel neglected become so demotivated they end up neglecting their customers. Brutalized employees produce brutalized customers.

It means if someone ever delighted *you* when you've been a customer somewhere, that individual was almost certainly duplicating the kind of treatment he or she routinely receives or sees demonstrated in his or her establishment. The way external customers are made to feel is almost infallibly a mirror image of the way internal customers are made to feel.

There's just no way around it: what the leadership in a business *does* will always have a far greater effect than anything it *says*. You're already leading by example—you need only make certain that your example is a good one, the one you want to see emulated throughout your business. If it's not, you've just identified a critical opportunity for improvement.

YOUR LEADERSHIP ON THE HOT SEAT

The time has come to ask a "leading" question: to what extent are you personally prepared to assume an active leadership role in the process of getting your business customer focused?

The chapters in Part II outline a Customer Focus Process step by step. The process entails one or more sessions where a team (or teams) of workers participates in a group activity

designed to generate ideas for producing happier customers. Someone has to lead these sessions—someone aware of
the process, sensitive to potential pitfalls, who by their very
presence will encourage participants to take the effort seriously and contribute to the best of their ability. Someone
like, say, the leader of the group.

In case it has somehow escaped your notice, I'm present-
ing you with a dandy little hot seat opportunity here. What
better way to demonstrate your personal commitment to
your vision than to personally get involved in helping your
workers make it a reality? (If you who are reading this are
actually the overseer of a vast far-flung business empire, far
removed from the daily goings-on down at the worker bee
level, you may not be the best candidate to preside at these
sessions. I would refer you to Chapter 12 for some suggestions on how to proceed in such a case.)

It's easy to imagine the kinds of objections that might
come immediately to mind: I'm no teacher. I don't know
how to run training sessions. (These are not training sessions; there is no teaching involved.) With my schedule, I
really don't have time to get involved in something like this.
(Let's just hope going out of business isn't eating up so much
of your precious time that there's none left over to *save* the
business.) I can't see myself standing up there trying to lead
them through some complicated procedure and getting all
balled up. (I'll walk you through the process step by step
in Part II; it's so simple even an executive can master it with
ease). If, after reading Part II and seeing for yourself what
a snap this process really is, you still feel a lingering compulsion to delegate the assignment to a more experienced
trainer or facilitator, please permit me to share a compulsion
of my own with you. I am compelled by conscience to advise
you that in my considerable experience with this process,
with businesses big and small, over a number of years, I
have observed a consistent pattern. The outcomes of the
sessions are always significantly less impressive whenever

someone *other* than the group's functional leader acts as facilitator—even when the substitute facilitator is as imposing a personage as the actual inventor of the process! The leadership-by-example element, the demonstration of a willingness to get personally involved, it seems, has a more positive impact on the results than any amount of facilitative razzle-dazzle.

As you read through Part II, I encourage you to picture yourself as the facilitator leading your people through the process; I'm hoping you'll recognize this as your opportunity *par excellence* to transmit some very powerful—and very positive—leadership signals to the people who make up your business.

Snappy Summary

▶ Put your customers to work as free consultants to advise on ways to improve your business.

▶ Put your customers to work as free goodwill ambassadors to spread positive word of mouth on your behalf.

▶ The business that does business more quickly does more business.

▶ The role of the leader is to *inspire others to follow*.

▶ The *mission* describes the leader's strategy for the business. A business without a mission is a business going nowhere.

▶ The *vision* depicts what successful accomplishment of the mission would look like. Ideally, it creates a moment of triumph that everyone can participate in and celebrate.

- ▶ The *commitment* has to be perceived as unshakeable. Everyone will watch to see if the leader is prepared to invest actual cold hard cash in pursuit of the vision.
- ▶ The *example* the leader sets, especially when his or her credibility is challenged, will inspire others to imitate what they see—whether it's good or bad.
- ▶ A particularly effective way to lead by example involves leading sessions of the Customer Focus Process itself.

II

THE CUSTOMER FOCUS PROCESS

Chapter Five

Mechanics of the Customer Focus Process

AVOIDING ACCIDENTAL EXCELLENCE

When a business routinely and consistently finds imaginative ways to exceed its customers' expectations, the customers often experience, along with the obvious sense of immediate delight, a deeper and longer-lasting feeling of appreciation: somebody, somewhere, had to care enough to go to the trouble of dreaming up such ideas. Where do these ideas come from? Customer-focused businesses seem somehow able to anticipate their customers' needs—they somehow know what will delight their customers. They manage to think of everything. How do they do it?

Let's face it: businesses don't just accidentally become consistent producers of happy customers, anymore than musicians accidentally become virtuosos or athletes accidentally become Olympic champions. In every field of human endeavor, where there is consistent excellence, it is only because a consistent effort has been made to achieve it. Superiority is arrived at by design, not by accident.

Note, though, that the athletes who set their sights on Olympic gold, and who push themselves the hardest in pursuit of that goal, somehow seem to end up deriving the most pleasure and gratification from athletics—even if ultimately they don't win the gold after all. Those musicians who discipline themselves to practice long and hard in order to qualify for careers on the concert stage are usually the ones for whom musicmaking becomes the greatest source of personal satisfaction—whether ultimately in the world's great concert halls or only in the front parlor. The businesses that "think of everything" are not the ones with employee morale problems; workers find the production of happy customers to be a personally rewarding activity.

Becoming very good at what we do requires an ongoing effort; *being* very good at what we do makes doing it an ongoing pleasure.

The Customer Focus Process (CFP) represents a disciplined, systematic way of becoming better at producing happy customers. Think of the techniques and approaches outlined below and in the chapters to come as the "effort" required to become better at what you do—even though, as you'll probably discover, it's an effort that can turn out to be quite pleasant and stimulating in itself.

Businesses with a strong customer focus remain in the minority, as we all know from bitter personal experience on the customer side of the counter. To make matters worse, many of the businesses that *do* manage to occasionally delight customers do so in sporadic, inconsistent, random ways. Their intermittent displays of customer attention are not the result of any disciplined, systematic approach; they occur only because individual employees or pockets of employees just happen to care enough to do what seems to be the right thing when circumstances permit. Such occasional flashes of excellence are, in short, not much more than happy accidents.

The practitioners of accidental excellence are in an extremely precarious situation. If, for whatever reason, the accidentally excellent employees happen to move on or simply become demotivated, *poof*—the firm's entire competitive advantage disappears.

The way to avoid this dangerous vulnerability is to transform the production of happy customers from an occasional happy accident to a formalized part of the way business is conducted. The Customer Focus Process provides a mechanism for accomplishing such a transformation.

SESSION OBSESSION

The **Customer Focus Process** is a technique for planning ways to produce happy customers. The actual planning is done in one or more meetings or sessions in which workers participate in a highly interactive brainstorming activity. (To keep things simple, I'll be describing the process as if there's to be only one session; see Chapter 12 for the whys and wherefores of multiple sessions.)

There is no fixed time duration for the session, though between three and four hours is typical. One facilitator will lead the session; participants may number from 2 to 20 or so. The participants should all belong to the same functional work group. In smaller businesses, this will mean the whole team; in larger organizations, it may mean the members of a department or division. (If the group numbers more than 25, better results may be obtained by splitting the group into two subgroups in separate sessions.) The session will be most successful if all members of the team can participate. This may necessitate scheduling the session after regular business hours; if so, I hope you won't hesitate to spring for pizza and beer, or in some other appropriate way give your workers an attractive incentive to donate some of their personal time. The outcome of this few hours of collective planning could very conceivably give your business a competitive advantage for quite some time to come; whatever money and energy you invest to help make the session a success is bound to yield significant returns.

STALKING AND CAPTURING THE WILD IDEA

When the brainstorming gets under way, ideas will start to fly. The facilitator's job is to ensure that all of these ideas are somehow captured and instantaneously displayed so that everyone can see them. As we'll see, the way the ideas are arrayed during the session can help stimulate innovative thinking and contribute to the development of more and better ideas. There are a number of ways to capture and display ideas for maximum effect.

When I'm facilitating the process, I give each participant a pad of 3M Post-it notes (two-by-three-inch size) and a smudgeproof felt-tip marker (such as Sanford's Sharpie marker) that produces heavy, highly legible writing. I prefer to have the participants sitting up nice and close, so I dispense with tables and provide clipboards (or just plain pieces of cardboard) to serve as writing surfaces. Each time a participant comes up with an idea, I have him or her write it on a Post-it in big print, and then I affix the Post-it to a blank flipchart, or to a whiteboard, or to the bare wall (if the surface is smooth enough for the Post-it to cling to it).

Some stationery stores sell bulletin boards that have been chemically treated to be adhesive; an example is 3M's 18-by-23-inch Post-it Bulletin Board. Also available in some stores are spray-on preparations that will render any smooth surface slightly adhesive. Either of these approaches will allow conventional slips of paper to be quickly and effortlessly posted for display. A slightly more cumbersome method involves giving participants file cards and enlisting the services of a helper to pin the completed cards to an appropriate surface (a bulletin board, if it's large enough, or even the side of a cloth-covered wall partition). The danger with this approach is once ideas start coming fast and furious, the pinner may have difficulty keeping up; valuable ideas may be lost in the scramble for pins. Also, if the position of several already-posted ideas must be changed to accommodate a new idea within the matrix, all of the ensuing unpinning and repinning may become tedious and time consuming.

With a little creativity, the reader can probably devise ingenious variations on these methods of capturing and displaying ideas if none of the above seem appropriate. Because I have personally found the Post-it technique so easy to work with, I'll be using that approach to describe the process in detail; this does not mean, however, that no other methods will work as well.

Whichever approach you decide to use, I encourage you to ensure that two elements are present. First, the participants should be writing down their own ideas; they will feel a greater sense of ownership in the process when, during and after the session, they can spot among the many Post-its on display those that bear their own ideas in their own handwriting. Second, the ideas have to be visible enough (and the participants have to be grouped near enough to the action) so that all ideas are readable by all participants at all times during the session.

If the final collection of written ideas is not to be affixed to an easily storable chart or sheet for future reference, I recommend that the whiteboard or wall surface used to hold the ideas be dedicated to the process—that is, that the ideas remain posted long after the session for later consultation. Even if there are to be no more follow-up sessions, ready access to the matrix paves the way for more of the generated ideas to be brought to fruition, as discussed in Chapter 12.

MATRIX TRICKS

To keep the display of ideas orderly and meaningful (especially for future reference), it is highly advisable that the ideas be posted in a logical arrangement of rows and columns. In such a matrix arrangement, various headings appear as upper rows, progressing from left to right; ideas that logically relate to these headings are then posted beneath them, in descending columns. The matrix will be even easier to read if headings appear on Post-its of a different color or at least are written in ink of a different color. The uppermost headings row shouldn't be positioned so high that participants cannot read it. Similarly, to avoid creating columns that extend downward to the floor, an arbitrary lower limit should be kept in mind; if a column of ideas reaches this lower limit and more ideas are still forthcoming, they should be posted in a new column to the right of the previous one. Thus, a single heading may spawn more than one vertical column of related ideas.

New columns progress from left to right across the chart or whiteboard or wall on which they're being affixed. The matrix becomes an expanding series of idea columns positioned roughly at participant eye level and extending from left to right like a train of interconnected box cars. And in these columns are strategies, ideas, activities that will enhance the customer experience and (if implemented) give your business a powerful competitive advantage.

KEEPING THE KETTLE BOILING

Throughout the CFP session, your goal as facilitator is to encourage creative thinking. You want each innovative new idea to trigger *more* new ideas. An important rule to impress upon your participants is that *they must state their idea out loud before writing it down on a Post-it.* This simple rule can help draw more and better ideas from the group in several ways.

As we'll see, the process is driven by a series of stimulating Key Questions from the facilitator; when these questions start unleashing a flood of ideas from participants, the danger exists that many of them will go unheard, unnoticed, unrecorded—and unimplemented. Chapter 8 outlines some techniques for keeping the flow of ideas under control, including enlisting the services of a helper to share the duties of capturing and posting ideas. In most cases, simply requiring participants to state their ideas aloud before writing them down slows the explosion of ideas just enough to ensure that everyone hears everyone else's ideas at the outset (without slowing things down *so* much that the momentum is lost). Thus, one idea stated aloud ("We could maybe give certain customers some kind of special discount") has an opportunity to trigger another ("Yeah, like maybe senior citizens, for example"), which may trigger another ("Hey, what if we made a certain day of the week Senior Citizens Day?") This ping-pong effect can often produce a final written idea (Senior Citizens Day) quite different than what would have initially been written (Discounts for Some Customers) if the initial idea had not been said aloud. Also, if in response to a question from the facilitator everyone just goes ahead and writes their respective answers down in silence, there will likely be several very similar ideas on paper and even some outright duplication. The facilitator will then need to sort through a batch of similar ideas; while he or she decides which ones belong in the matrix, the creative part of the process grinds to a halt.

An effective procedure for transferring ideas to the matrix would follow steps such as these:

1. Encourage one of the participants to share his or her idea aloud. (Invite comments from the others as appropriate, ensuring the idea is in no way ridiculed or trivialized.)

2. Ask the participant to summarize his or her idea on a Post-it.

3. While that idea is being written down, ask a second participant to share aloud his or her idea. (Again, invite comments as appropriate.)

4. Ask the second participant to write his or her idea on a Post-it.

5. While the second idea is being written down, take the completed Post-it from the first participant and affix it under the appropriate heading in the matrix.

6. Ask a third participant to share his or her idea. (Invite comments.) Ask the participant to write the idea on a Post-it.

7. Affix the second participant's Post-it to the matrix.

8. Ask a fourth participant to share his or her idea. (Or, if there is no fourth participant, ask the first participant to share another of his or her ideas.)

And so on, until all ideas have been heard, written down, and added to the matrix. In this way the transfer of ideas to the matrix does not interrupt the flow of new ideas.

The procedure takes longer to read about than to actually perform. It may seem clumsy or complicated on the printed page, but in practice it quickly becomes a very natural rhythm that keeps the process moving at a brisk pace and tends to generate enthusiasm and a sense of fun among participants.

CUSTOMER FOCUS PROCESS OVERVIEW

The remaining chapters will lead you through the CFP terrain step by step; but before we begin exploring at ground level, here's a quick aerial reconnaissance of the landscape.

The Customer Focus Process is divided into phases. After appropriate opening remarks to get the session under way, the preliminary phase begins; participants identify the different *customer categories* they do business with. They then enumerate those *customer expectations* that are unique to each of these separate categories of customers. (This activity is described in detail in Chapter 6.)

Next, participants break a typical customer transaction down into the actual sequence of events the customer goes through; defining this *transaction sequence* brings the preliminary phase to a close (Chapter 7).

The bulk of the CFP session comprises three brainstorming phases, each linked to one of three customer focus principles.

In Phase One, participants review the transaction sequence and brainstorm ideas for *exceeding customer expectations* at each individual step in the sequence (Chapter 8).

Phase Two also involves reviewing the steps in the transaction sequence; this time participants brainstorm ideas for *making customers feel important* at each step (Chapter 9).

In Phase Three, participants review the expectations they earlier assigned to various customer categories and brainstorm ideas for addressing these unique expectations, thereby *tailoring the experience to fit the customer* (Chapter 10).

The CFP session concludes with the facilitator recording in an *action log* any voluntary commitments participants make to take action on one or more of the ideas generated in the brainstorming phases (Chapter 11). This makes it easier for the facilitator to track progress and celebrate successes in a *follow-up meeting* (Chapter 12).

BUILDING A BETTER LEMONADE STAND

Whether your business sells state-of-the-art, high-yield, self-calibrating, pulse-resistant, multiapplication, micronetwork-driven, electrodigital magnetic converters, or oven mitts bearing a picture of a cow, the basic challenges that confront you are much the same. Greater competitive pressure, higher customer expectations, lower employee morale— these are issues virtually *all* businesses are grappling with.

When I meet managers or executives of a new client organization for the first time, one thing I will almost invariably hear is, "Let me give you a little background on our business to help you appreciate how different and unique our situation is." I will then be given a detailed overview that boils down to the fact that they're struggling with greater competitive pressure, higher customer expectations, and lower employee morale. Most businesses believe their problems are unique; this naive notion is just one more problem they all have in common.

As I walk you through the CFP session step by step, I'll be describing the proceedings as if we're members of a work team in an imaginary business. To keep things simple, I've chosen a very simple business for us to be a part of—a lemonade stand. It could have been a dentist's office, or a distributor of plumbing fixtures, or a retailer of frilly underthings; it could have been any sort of business. But since the big issues (and the best ways of dealing with them) would all be pretty similar, I prefer to use as familiar and uncomplicated a business as possible. After all, in an operation as basic as a lemonade stand, just how much scope *is* there to enhance the customer experience? The customer approaches the stand, buys the lemonade, and departs. No telephones, no order forms, no invoices, no delivery options, none of the many opportunities more complicated businesses have to exceed customer excpectations. If even as bare-bones a business as this can find ways to focus on the customer and outshine the competition, imagine the wealth of opportunities to do the same that can be uncovered in more conventional enterprises.

So, now let me give you a little background on our business to help you appreciate how different and unique our situation is.

Our lemonade stand has a reputation for serving delicious, refreshing lemonade. We're also fortunate to be situated in a good spot—on a busy sidewalk near a shopping center, in the cool shade of trees at the edge of a nearby park. There's also a construction site across the street, with hordes of thirsty workers. In short, we have it made. Or rather we *did*, until some neighborhood kids recently opened a stand of their own not far from ours. Unfortunately, they too are in a shady location. And, unfortunately, they too are selling good lemonade; indeed, people really can't tell ours from theirs. To make things worse, they're charging *less* for theirs. Our sales have really begun to fall off. We've decided we have to do something. We can't do much to improve our already good-as-it-can-be lemonade, so we've decided we're going to compete by improving the experience customers have when they frequent our stand.

The following chapters outline the process we'll follow to determine how best to accomplish this.

Snappy Summary

▶ Becoming very good at what we do requires an ongoing effort; *being* very good at what we do makes doing it an ongoing pleasure.

▶ The Customer Focus Process can transform the production of happy customers from an occasional accident to a formalized part of the way business is conducted.

▶ The facilitator's job is to ensure that all ideas generated in the session are instantaneously captured and displayed.

▶ The participants must state their ideas out loud before writing them down.

▶ All posted ideas should be readable by all participants at all times during the session.

Chapter Six

Defining Customer Categories

NOT ALL CUSTOMERS ARE CREATED EQUAL

In our lemonade stand, as in any business, our primary objective is (or should be) the production of happy customers. Customer happiness is linked directly to customer expectations and the extent to which our business consistently meets or, better yet, exceeds them. The logical place to begin our Customer Focus Process (CFP) session, therefore, is with identifying the expectations of our customers. And immediately we encounter our first opportunity to differentiate ourselves from the competition.

There are certain *general* expectations that all our customers share: promptness, accuracy, courtesy, high-quality goods and services at reasonable prices, and so on. Most businesses think of these types of things when their thoughts turn to customer expectations. But these are really only the tip of the expectations iceberg.

Beyond these general expectations there usually exists a whole range of expectations that are *specific* to certain categories of customers. Most businesses miss the boat altogether in this regard. Not all customers share the same expectations; if we can isolate these specific expectations and start doing some things to better meet or exceed them, we will almost certainly begin positioning ourselves in customers' eyes as the better alternative. The Preliminary Phase of the CFP session begins with uncovering those specific expectations that apply to specific categories of customers.

OPENING REMARKS

At some point you're going to have to explain to your participants the basic what, why, and how of the process. It can be done before the session, orally or in writing, as part of the notification regarding place and time for the session. Or it can be done at the outset of the session itself. It can be as brief or as elaborate as you wish. But at the very least, it should contain the following elements:

- The reasons you feel there's a need to improve the customer experience.
- How the participants' ideas will be captured during the session.
- The fact that participants will not be required to take action on any ideas generated in the session, though they will be free to do so voluntarily if they choose.

This last point is especially critical. If participants perceive the session as a condescending way to make them feel *they're* the source of customer dissatisfaction, if they sense that you view this as a glorious opportunity for them to smarten up and start doing things properly, the session will be doomed to failure from the start. They need to be assured that they can let their imaginations soar without worrying that anything they come up with can and will be used against them.

This is one of the main points facilitator Sandy Best covers in her opening remarks to the team at Best Lemonade.

Sandy: Good morning, group. As you know, that lemonade stand down the street has been hurting our business lately. The purpose of this session is to try and come up with some ideas that will help us compete more effectively. We'll be focusing on trying to make the whole experience of coming to our stand more pleasant for the customer than going to their stand.

We'll be using Post-it notes to record our ideas. At the end of the session, some of you may decide to take on one or more of the ideas as personal action items; if so, we'll keep a record of that fact and follow up at a later date to see how well they've worked. Please understand, however, the fact that you write an idea down does not mean you're expected to take it on as an action item later. We just want to get your creative juices going, see what kind of ideas we can come up when we all put our heads together.

PRELIMINARY PHASE, FIRST SECTION: CUSTOMER CATEGORIES

You're now going to get the participants to think about the different types of customers they interact with. Specifically, you're looking for those categories that make up a significant proportion of your customer base and that might have expectations applying only to that particular category.

The written answers you receive in this section will each constitute a heading for a separate column in the matrix; the relevant expectations will then be posted beneath the appropriate customer category heading. If you'd like matrix headings to appear in a different color, you may want to consider writing all identified customer categories yourself, on Post-its of your color, and then letting the participants fill in each column with relevant expectations recorded on Post-its of their color.

MATRIX MAP I
Headings: Customer Categories

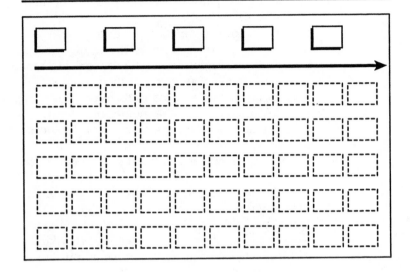

These customer categories should be posted as a row of headings extending from left to right across the top line of the matrix, as indicated by the solid boxes above. (Note that the headings are spaced far enough apart to permit two columns of Post-its to be positioned beneath each, as indicated by dotted lines; this is to avoid ending up with long columns that extend to the floor. If your group numbers more than 12 participants, it may even be advisable to allow space for *three* columns under each heading.)

> **Sandy:** Team, if we're going to dream up ideas to exceed customer expectations at our lemonade stand, we should start by making sure we know what our customers' expectations are. But because different kinds of customers may expect different things, let's begin by asking ourselves, "Are there separate categories of customers that

come to our stand, with separate kinds of expectations?" I'd like to hear your answers out loud: what are the main kinds of customers we get?

▶ *KEY QUESTION 1*

What different categories of customers do we do business with?

Mary: Well, we get a lot of construction workers.

Sandy: Okay, good. I'm going to write Construction Workers on this pink Post-it and put it right up here. What other kinds of customers?

Barry: Kids.

Sandy: Good. Kids—I'll write that down and put it up here beside Construction Workers. What other kinds?

Terry: Joggers, in the park?

Sandy: Sure, that's a good one. I'll write that down. Who else comes to our stand?

Larry: We get a lot of older folks.

Sandy: All right, let me make a note of that. Who else?

Sherry: Teenagers.

Perry: Shoppers carrying packages.

Cary: People with pets.

Sandy: Not too fast, I—

Gary: Italians in wheelchairs.

Harry: Lady wrestlers.

Sandy: Okay, please, not too fast, I want to get all these down. Gary, you said?

Gary: Italians in wheelchairs.

Sandy: All right, now, let me ask you—would you say we get a lot of Italians in wheelchairs?

Gary: Well, maybe not a lot, but we did have one a couple of weeks ago.

Sandy: I think for the purposes of today's session I'd like to focus particularly on those kinds of customers who make up the bulk of our clientele. What about people in wheelchairs generally—do we get a fair number of those?

Gary: Naw, not really. There was just that one.

Sandy: Okay. And Harry, you mentioned one category.

Harry: Nothing. Forget it.

Sandy: All right, did I get everybody's? Okay, let's look at who we've identified as our main types of customers. We've got Construction Workers, Kids, Joggers, Older Folks, Teenagers, Shoppers with Packages, and People with Pets. Have we left anybody out?

The question will tend to come up: just how narrow should these categories be? Is "joggers" specific enough, or should we distinguish between male and female joggers, older and younger joggers, with and without eyeglasses, and so on. As a rule of thumb, a general category like joggers is usually sufficiently specific to allow relevant expectations to be identified. The exception would be a lemonade stand that sets up shop next door to the Meadowvale Home For Elderly Vision-Impaired Lady Joggers. In other words, the real determining factor is numbers: unless a proposed sub-category represents a significant proportion of the total customer base, it can probably be considered part of the main category.

The session will be easier to manage if fewer than 10 categories make it into the matrix. Do not discourage your participants if they come up with more, however; continue to capture the categories until there are no more to be had. Then divide the total in half and work with one group of categories (preferably the most common) in this session and the remainder in a second session at some future date. If the group comes up with more than 20 distinct customer categories (which is unlikely), a third session may be in order.

Unskilled facilitators have a tendency to rephrase participants' ideas: "Larry mentioned older people—I'll make a note of Senior Citizens right here." It's preferable to use the participants' own words whenever possible. Exceptions would be if the original wording were inappropriate ("Harry, rather than Old Buzzards, how about if we put down Older Folks?") or too long ("Terry, there may not be room to write 'Health Nuts Who Won't Drink Anything Unless They Can First Read a Label Listing Every Ingredient Used' on a Post-it; what if you wrote Health-Conscious People?")

Throughout the CFP session, no doubt ideas will pop into the facilitator's mind that he or she will want to see added to the matrix. It is generally not a good idea for the facilitator to start adding his or her own ideas to a collection of ideas generated by the team ("Hey, we also get postal workers at our stand—I'd better add that category to the matrix.") The danger with this approach is that it deprives participants of one of the most attractive features of the CFP: their sense of *ownership* over the contents of the matrix. This sense of ownership makes it easier for them at the end of the session to voluntarily take on one or more improvement ideas as personal action items. A more effective approach for facilitators is to use prompts and questions that will help the team come up with the idea on their own: "Do we get any types of customers who walk past our stand every day? Any kinds of delivery people, for example?"

PRELIMINARY PHASE, SECOND SECTION: CUSTOMER EXPECTATIONS

Think of each posted customer category as the heading of a column; under each heading we're now going to capture the unique expectations that pertain to the particular category in question.

Post-it notes have a tendency to curl away slightly from the surface to which they've been affixed; to minimize clutter and maximize legibility in the matrix, I always encourage participants to orient all their Post-its the same way on their writing surfaces (such as, adhesive edge to the left). The result will be rows and columns of Post-its all curling in the same direction.

In facilitating this section of the process, you may occasionally need to remind participants of the distinction between *expectations* and *innovations*. For example, in answer to the question "What kinds of expectations do kids who come to our lemonade stand have?", responses may begin with things like, Patience while they count out their money, or We don't talk down to them. As ideas continue to emerge, however, the character of some of them may begin to subtly change: We hand out free balloons. A tape of children's songs plays in the background. We could dress up like circus clowns. In their eagerness to begin brainstorming ideas to delight customers, participants will often jump ahead to that activity prematurely, without even realizing it. The way to get them back on track is to remind them what the word "expectation" really means: something the customer expects to see or have happen; something that, if it's absent, will cause *disappointment* for the customer. If, when you're fishing for expectations, participants instead tend to give you innovations, there are two things you should do. First, if the innovation sounds like a good idea, have them write it down anyway; we don't want to lose any good ideas. (You can put the written idea aside temporarily and add it to the matrix later among other innovative ideas.) Second, in as tactful a manner as possible, challenge the participant(s): "Would you say that's something this type of customer actually expects? Would this customer be disappointed if we didn't do that?" This sort of gentle reminder will usually succeed in putting the focus back on actual expectations.

MATRIX MAP 2
Entries: Customer Expectation

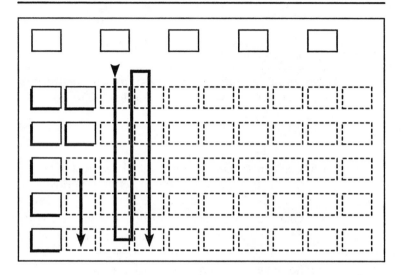

The need for tact, throughout the process, is great. You want to avoid making participants feel they've given a wrong answer; this will only create embarrassment and inhibit them from offering more ideas. When you offer a challenge to an answer, your manner should suggest that you're almost not too sure yourself whether the answer should go into the matrix or not; it's as if you're asking them to help you make up your mind about it.

It will now be appropriate to have participants write their own answers on their own Post-its in their own color. These Post-its will be added to the matrix beneath the relevant heading, as indicated by the shaded boxes above.

> **Sandy:** We're now going to see if we can identify some expectations that are unique to each of these customer categories. Our first category is Construction Workers. I'd like to hear your

answers out loud, please. What kind of
expectations do construction workers who come
to our stand have?

▶ *Key Question 2*

*What kinds of unique expectations do [customers
of a particular category] have when they do
business with us?*

Barry: Well, their breaks aren't very long, so I'd say
        they expect us to be able to serve them fast.
        They don't want to have to wait in a long line.

Sandy: Okay, that's an important one. Could I get you
        to write that down on a Post-it? I'll put it up
        here under Construction Workers.

Barry: So, what am I supposed to write down?

Sandy: Well, you said they expect us to serve them fast,
        so why don't you just put down Fast Service?
        And please print it nice and large, so it's easy to
        read. While he does that, do any of you have
        other ideas about the expectations construction
        workers have?

Terry: Lots of ice.

Sandy: Good! Please jot that down. What else?

Mary: Big portions—they're thirsty!

Larry: Carry-out cartons, so they can take their drink
        back with them.:

Perry: Maybe we could even carry their drinks right
        out to their site for them! They wouldn't even
        have to cross the street at all!

Sandy: Okay, I want to make sure we capture all of
        these terrific ideas. Mary, you said Big
        Portions—please jot that down. And Larry,
        yours was Carry-Out Cartons, am I right? Please

write that down. Now Perry suggested we deliver their drinks right to their work site. My question is, would you say that's something they actually expect from us?

Perry: I think they'd love it!

Sandy: So do I! It's a fantastic idea! If you write it down, I'll put aside for later, when we start getting into innovations. For right now, though, I want to make sure we concentrate on the expectations our construction workers have. Any more ideas?

Terry: Well, when they come over on their break, they expect us to have fresh lemonade that's made and ready for them.

Sandy: Absolutely! We have to anticipate their breaks and make sure we have enough in stock for them when they arrive. Please make a note of that.

Experienced facilitators are generous with praise: "That's good, Perry; please write that one down." "Wow! Excellent idea, Mary!" They know how this kind of frequent positive reinforcement encourages further contributions from participants.

When we have listed all of our major categories of customers and identified their unique expectations, we're ready to begin breaking a typical customer experience down into its component steps; that's the third and final section of the Preliminary Phase, which comes next.

Snappy Summary

▶ Opening remarks should cover (1) reasons for the need to improve, (2) how ideas will be captured, and (3) the voluntary nature of the process.

▶ Whenever possible, transfer participants' own words to the matrix.

▶ Clarify the distinction between expectations and innovations.

▶ Be generous with praise for participants' ideas.

▶ Key Question 1: *What different categories of customers do we do business with?*

▶ Key Question 2: *What kinds of unique expectations do [customers of a particular category] have when they do business with us?*

Chapter Seven

The Transaction Sequence

MAPPING OUT THE CUSTOMER EXPERIENCE

By uncovering our customers' expectations (as in the previous chapter), we have identified some of the "construction materials" we'll be using to build an improved customer experience. But just as in renovating a house, we need more than raw materials for actual construction to begin. There must be a blueprint, some sort of plan, that documents the shape and dimensions of the existing structure and specifies where and how to incorporate the new construction into the old.

The underlying structure of the existing customer experience must be similarly mapped out before changes can be made and new elements added in any systematic way. The Preliminary Phase of the Customer Focus Process (CFP) concludes, then, with identification of the various steps that make up the total customer experience.

Some businesses (such as a lemonade stand) provide customers with a simple, straightforward experience that lasts only for a few minutes. Some (such as a university) provide complex experiences that entail many decision-points and optional elements and that can take years to unfold in their entirety. It might be a little unrealistic for a team of university administrators to imagine that a few hours spent shuffling Post-it notes will result in a clear plan of action for overhauling every aspect of the university's operations. To keep the scope of the CFP session within manageable bounds, it makes sense to limit its purview to a single component of the customer experience: one typical *transaction*.

At a lemonade stand a typical transaction (customer buys lemonade) may represent 95 percent of the total customer experience; a typical university transaction (student enrolls in classes) may account for only 2 percent of the total experience. For the purposes of selecting a typical transaction for CFP analysis, the proportion of the total experience represented by a particular type of transaction is not the most critical criterion. More important are the answers you give to the following three questions:

- Does this particular type of transaction typically generate a significant amount of customer dissatisfaction?
- Would improving this particular type of transaction give our business a significant competitive advantage?
- Would improving this particular type of transaction make life a lot more pleasant for a significant proportion of our external and internal customers?

If you can think of a typical transaction that earns three easy "yes" answers to these questions, you've identified a good candidate for a CFP session. If you have no difficulty thinking of *several* types of transaction that can easily earn three "yes" answers, it simply means you may want to consider planning for more than one CFP session in the months ahead. The three questions can help you prioritize your transactions. If more than one generates dissatisfaction, which generates *most*? If improving more than one would give you a competitive advantage, which would give you *most*? Which, if improved, would simplify life *most*? The transaction that scores the most "mosts" wins the right to be subjected to CFP scrutiny first, with the others ranked in descending order from most to least.

Why a "typical" transaction? Because there's little to be gained by improving a transaction that creates misery for customers whenever it happens if it only happens once every fifth leap year—especially if another generates nearly as much customer anguish and happens every five minutes of every business day. Frequency of occurrence should be one of the main selection criteria. If several different transactions score about equally when answering the three questions above, frequency should become *the* most important issue.

Selection of the transaction is the facilitator's responsibility; it's advisable to come to the CFP session with that decision finalized.

PRELIMINARY PHASE, THIRD SECTION: STEPS IN THE TRANSACTION SEQUENCE

Once the participants have been advised of the particular transaction they're going to be working on in a session, they must identify the individual steps that constitute the typical sequence of events in this type of transaction.

The first step is to determine what constitutes the first step. Where in this particular transaction sequence does the customer enter the scene?

Participants will sometimes offer, "Customer walks in the door" as a first step in the transaction sequence. Then someone else will say, "Wait, it actually begins when they drive up and park in our parking lot." Someone else will say, "No, it starts even before that—they call to ask if we have the product they want in stock before they drive over." "Hold on," someone else will say, "It begins when they read about our product in one of our flyers. That's where they get our phone number." "Before then—it starts when they first learn to read." "When they start school." "Are born." "Parents get married." "Grandparents come over from the old world." "Adam and Eve."

Where *does* a transaction sequence begin? As a rule of thumb, the first step should usually reflect the first *contact point* with the customer. It's the customer's first opportunity to form an impression about the kind of experience we're about to deliver. It *may* be a phone call. It *may* be when he or she is parking out front (especially if our parking lot has potholes deep enough to swallow a small European car). It's that moment that represents our first opportunity to make things better for the customer. This, for the purposes of our CFP session, is where the transaction sequence begins. And it similarly ends at our final opportunity to improve things for the customer. So now—what comes in between?

In the interests of being thorough, participants will sometimes dissect the transaction sequence into slices so thin dozens of steps are required just to reach the point where the customers sets foot on our premises. Customers don't simply "telephone to verify that item is in stock." They "pick up the handset" and "verify that the dial tone is present"; if not, they "hang up and try again later." Once they get the dial tone, they proceed to "dial the number," an operation fraught with opportunities for error, each of which would require starting all over again, and so on. It may be appropriate for you, as facilitator, to help the group break down the transaction sequence into a manageable number of steps. The rule of thumb here is that a total of 10 steps is usually about right. Anything more than 15 starts becoming unwieldy; it may mean we're slicing too thinly—or that there's actually more than one transaction sequence being lumped together. (If so, determine the end point of the first, and defer the other(s) to a later session.)

The steps that make up the transaction sequence are going to form another row of headings along the top of the matrix, like the Customer Categories earlier. Though you want to encourage maximum participation and involvement from the members of your team, it's appropriate for you to write down their headings ideas in your color. This will later make it easier for them to distinguish the headings from the entries bearing their brainstormed ideas, which occupy the bulk of the matrix. In so doing, you have the opportunity to gently and diplomatically impose your own view of the magnitude of each step in the sequence: "To ensure that we'll have enough time in this session to examine the entire transaction sequence, I'm going to suggest we lump all these telephone activities into one heading, "Customer Phones to Verify Item Is in Stock." (Note that imposing your own wording or ideas in this way is *only* appropriate when generating *headings*, and even then should be used only as a last resort. Such an approach is extremely counterproductive once participants begin offering ideas for entries beneath the headings.)

As with the earlier Customer Categories headings, it's advisable to space these headings out as indicated in Matrix Map 3, with room for at least two columns beneath each.

Sandy: Okay, team, we've identified the major categories of customers that visit our lemonade stand, and the key expectations of each; now we're going to look at a typical transaction these customers go through when they come to our stand, and we're going to break the transaction down into the various steps the customer goes through. So what would you say are the steps that make up a typical customer transaction at our stand? How does the transaction begin?

MATRIX MAP 3
Headings: Steps in the Transaction Sequence

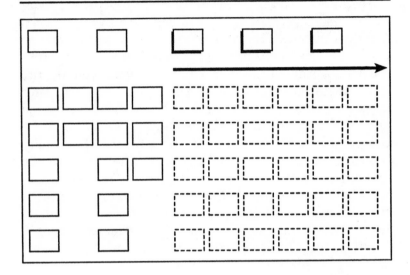

▶ *Key Question 3*

What are the various steps our customers typically go through as part of [this particular type of transaction]?

Terry: The customer buys a cup of lemonade.

Sandy: All right, now, let's think about this. Is that where the transaction actually begins, or is there something that comes before that?

Terry: Oh, okay, I see what you mean. First the customer has to get thirsty. Then he buys a cup of lemonade.

Sandy: But is getting thirsty really part of the transaction? We want to pinpoint when our customer has his or her first contact with our stand.

Terry: Ah. So he walks up to the stand. Is that where it begins?

Sandy: What do the rest of you think?

Larry: It starts when he sees the stand.

Mary: Or maybe he's in the neighborhood, and he thinks about the stand because he's thirsty and he stopped here once before and he liked it.

Perry: Or else maybe he just hears about the stand the night before while he's playing poker with his cousin and a bunch of the guys from the welding shop.

Sandy: We're looking for a typical customer's first actual encounter with the stand.

Larry: He sees the stand.

Sandy: Everyone agree with that? All right, I'll put down as a heading, Customer Sees the Stand. What comes next?

Terry: He buys a cup of lemonade.

Gary: Wait. First he has to tell us what he wants, right?

Mary: But doesn't he first have to walk up to the stand?

Barry: Hold it—first wouldn't he have to check and make sure he's got enough money in his pocket?

Gary: Plus wouldn't he have to check his watch, make sure he has time to stop for a cup of lemonade?

Sandy: We're listing the steps in an actual transaction; it means the customer has already decided to do business with us. So what happens after he first sees the stand?

Terry: He buys a cup of lemonade.

Mary: I still say he has to walk up to the stand first.

Sandy: Okay, I'll write that down. Then?

Terry: He buys a cup of lemonade.

Gary: Don't we greet him first?

Sandy: Team?

Barry: We greet him, yes. Then he places his order.

Sandy: All right, I'll get both of those down.

Terry: Then does he buy his cup of lemonade?

Barry: I'd say then we hand him his order.

Larry: And he pays for it.

Mary: Right. We give him what he ordered, he gives us the money.

Sandy: Let me get those two steps down.

Barry: We give him change, if there's any due.

Sandy: Okay, We Make Change.

Mary: And he leaves.

Sandy: Customer Leaves. Okay, let's review what we've got: Customer Sees the Stand, Customer Approaches Stand, We Greet Customer, Customer Places Order, We Give Customer What Was Ordered, Customer Pays, We Make Change, and Customer Leaves. That's great, team. I think that pretty well covers everything.

Terry: When I was saying, Customer Buys a Cup of Lemonade, this is what I meant.

With customer categories, customer expectations, and the steps in a typical transaction sequence all identified and posted in the matrix, the Preliminary Phase of the CFP session is complete. The team is now ready to give their creativity free rein.

Snappy Summary

▶ A transaction sequence is a series of approximately 10 steps that summarize what the customer typically experiences in a particular type of transaction.

▶ Those types of transactions that happen *most often*, generate *most customer dissatisfaction* and, if improved, will give the *most competitive advantage* and have the *most beneficial effect* on external and internal customers are the types most eligible for CFP analysis.

▶ The beginning and ending points for any transaction sequence are the first and final contact points with the customer.

▶ Key Question 3: *What are the various steps our customers typically go through as part of [this particular type of transaction]?*

Chapter Eight

Customer Focus Process, Phase One

A MATTER OF PRINCIPLES

The three creative brainstorming phases of the Customer Focus Process (CFP) are driven by three core principles. Not only do these three principles summarize the basic philosophy of customer focus, they also provide a convenient roadmap for facilitators of the process. Each of the core principles calls to mind a related Key Question participants will be asked in the CFP session—and it is the answers to these particular questions that fill the matrix with creative and innovative ideas for improving the customer experience.

The Customer Focus Principles

1. **Exceed the customer's expectations every step of the way.**
2. **Make the customer feel important.**
3. **Tailor the experience to fit the customer.**

Because you will have several opportunities to allude to these three core principles in the remainder of the session, you may find it helpful to transcribe them to a flipchart or whiteboard for easy reference.

Our objective as a CFP facilitator is to give our participants an opportunity to engage in some creative thinking and generate some innovative ideas related to all three of these core principles. As in any form of brainstorming, our initial purpose is to stimulate and capture ideas. This is therefore *not* the time to evaluate the ideas in terms of their feasibility, or to discuss if, when, how, or why they should or shouldn't be implemented. Such considerations come later, once all three brainstorming phases are complete. Even the most outlandish and impractical ideas, if proposed in earnest by a participant, should be included in the matrix. An outrageous idea from one participant has a way of inspiring a similar—but much more practical—variation from another, a useful idea that might otherwise never have come to light if the original "outrageous" notion had not been posted.

TAKING A DRINK FROM NIAGARA

It is typical of CFP sessions to suddenly accelerate dramatically in pace once the Preliminary Phase is complete and the creative floodgates can finally be thrown open in the first brainstorming phase.

The challenge for the facilitator becomes one of control: ensuring all ideas are spoken aloud before being written down, ensuring all ideas *are* written down, ensuring all written ideas are transferred to the matrix. In larger groups made up of highly motivated and enthusiastic participants, the facilitator is in considerable danger of being buried alive under a mountain of sticky Post-it notes.

One effective way to stay ahead of the torrent of ideas involves enlisting the services of a helper. In most groups there'll be at least one shy individual more reluctant to contribute ideas than the rest; solicit his or her help in collecting Post-its and affixing them to the matrix. Getting reluctant participants involved in this way not only lightens your workload when things start moving at a faster pace than you can handle alone, it may also reduce their inhibitions and encourage them to begin adding ideas of their own. Conversely, you may find yourself with a particularly vocal participant who enjoys being the center of attention and tends to dominate the interactive phases of the process. Assigning this individual the task of "managing the matrix" keeps him or her pleasantly occupied while making it easier for all the others to make their ideas heard.

If you're fortunate enough to have such an enthusiastic group that even the efforts of a helper aren't sufficient to keep up with the flood of good ideas, it may be necessary for you to periodically slow things down a little. Skill is required to do this in a way that doesn't dampen enthusiasm or curtail the creativity of the group. Any time it becomes necessary to put on the brakes, your manner should make it clear you're *delighted* with their outpouring of ideas, not frustrated by your inability to keep up with it. Something along these lines is appropriate: "Wow, so many great ideas—please don't forget any of them while I try to get all of your Post-its up on the matrix." By comparison, the following should be avoided: "Could you please slow *down* for a minute? How on earth do you expect me to get all these ideas posted if you keep spitting them out so fast?" The purpose of the CFP is to generate innovative ideas. Being suddenly confronted with more than you can handle may be a problem, but it's a very nice problem to have.

PHASE ONE: EXCEEDING EXPECTATIONS

All that has come before in the session has been preparatory. In Phase One we initiate the first round of creative brainstorming by applying Core Principle 1 to each of the identified steps in the transaction sequence under review. We invite participants to share their ideas aloud; if appropriate, we ask them to summarize their idea on a Post-it note. If the idea needs clarification or refining, we encourage discussion about it with the group until there is general agreement about how (if at all) the idea should be described in writing. In the rare event that the idea is simply totally inappropriate, we explain why as positively and diplomatically as possible, and move on to other ideas.

MATRIX MAP 4
Exceeding Customer Expectations

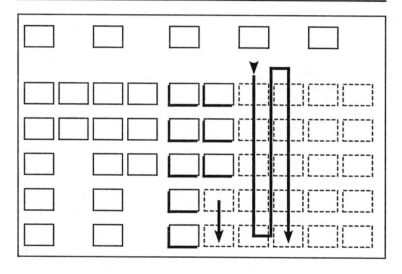

Post-it notes bearing ideas for ways to exceed customer expectations are posted as descending columns beneath the matrix heading, which describes the relevant step in the transaction, as indicated above.

Experienced facilitators use a technique called "bridging" to help prevent participants from losing a sense of where they are in a given session or process. They create a bridge between what has come before and what is about to take place by reviewing the material just covered and explaining how what comes next relates to it.

Sandy: We've identified all the steps in a typical customer transaction at our lemonade stand. We're now ready to begin Phase One of our creative brainstorming. To help us do that, we're going to review the first of three Customer Focus Principles. It says, "Exceed the customer's expectations every step of the way." So what we're going to do now is think of ways to apply this first principle to each step in our transaction sequence. We said the first step was, Customer Sees Stand. So what could we do that would exceed our customers' expectations when they first see our stand?

▶ KEY QUESTION 4
_____

What could be done [in each step of the transaction sequence] to exceed our customers' expectations?

Terry: Give them a special free lemonade deal!

Barry: We get dressed up like cartoon characters!

Sandy: Okay, Terry suggested a free-lemonade promotional offer. But Terry, can we give them that kind of deal if they're just seeing the stand from a distance? Remember, we don't greet them until two steps later.

Terry: All right then, how about a big "free lemonade" sign you can see from far way? That'll pull them in!

Jerry: It'll pull them in, except we'll go broke.

Sandy: Let's not evaluate the ideas—we're just brainstorming at this point. Please go ahead, Terry, and write your idea down.

Terry: I'll just write Big Sign to Attract Customers.

> **Perry:** We could put up colorful streamers like they do in used car lots or something.
>
> **Mary:** Balloons.
>
> **Sandy:** Good. Please write those ideas down. But Barry, didn't you have an idea?
>
> **Barry:** I said we could dress up like cartoon characters.
>
> **Larry:** Wouldn't we roast alive in those things, though?
>
> **Sandy:** No evaluation—let's just get the ideas up onto the matrix. Please write that one down, Barry.
>
> **Gary:** I got one. When we give change, let's round it off in their favor so they don't get pennies.
>
> **Sandy:** That's excellent, Gary. Now since we're not up to the We Make Change step yet, if you write that down I'll post it under that heading. For the moment let's continue focusing on our first step, when customers first see the stand.

There are really no wrong answers in the brainstorming phases of the CFP other than ideas that are clearly offensive ("Let's put up a sign that says, No People with Stupid-Looking Hair Allowed.") or dangerous ("What about a sign that says Sword-Swallowing Contest—Big Prizes?") As mentioned earlier, even wildly impractical ideas ("Let's ask the city if we can move our stand right up to the edge of the curb so traffic in the right-hand lane can stop and order lemonade from inside the vehicle like at those fast-food drive-through deals.") can inspire innovative and workable variations ("Let's create a side counter at our stand and call it a drive-through for kids on bikes.") It's always better to put up an idea that goes nowhere than to miss one that might have inspired the innovation of the decade.

> **Sandy:** Any more ideas for exceeding customer expectations when they first see our stand? Jerry?
>
> **Jerry:** I can't think of any more.

Sandy: All right, let's move to our second step,
Customer Approaches Stand. How could we
exceed their expectations as they approach?"

Sherry: Maybe they could hear nice happy music
playing.

Sandy: Great idea! Please write that down. What else?

Terry: I've got one. They hear an announcement over a
loudspeaker: "Free lemonade! Come and get it!"

Jerry: Except we'll go broke!

Sandy: Maybe we don't have to specify what the
message is right now. How about just putting
down, Exciting Announcement over
Loudspeaker.

After just a few minutes of this sort of brainstorming, the
matrix will begin to fill up with interesting ideas, some of
which would be quite easy and painless to implement (We
greet every customer with a big friendly smile. We always
apologize for the delay if a customer had to wait to be
served.) It's natural for the group to wonder, perhaps even
aloud, Why haven't we been doing this all along? or Why
has nobody ever thought of this before?

Such questions are a healthy indicator that the group is
already becoming more customer-focused and is recognizing that such a focus has been lacking in the past. It isn't
really useful, however, to bring the session to a standstill in
order to formally begin discussing these kinds of issues. A
quick "maybe we didn't always appreciate the importance
of such matters—that's precisely why we're participating in
this session today" should be sufficient to permit the flow
of creative ideas to resume.

By the time the last step in the transaction sequence has
been subjected to Key Question 4 and all answers are up in
the matrix, the group may feel that their collective pool of
imaginative ideas has been drained dry. But give them a
coffee break and lots of positive reinforcement for the work

they've done so far, and they'll be ready to proceed to the next phase of brainstorming.

Snappy Summary

▶ The Customer Focus Principles:
  1. Exceed the customer's expectations every step of the way.
  2. Make the customer feel important.
  3. Tailor the experience to fit the customer.
▶ If brainstormed ideas flow more quickly than you can deal with, enlist the services of a helper to "manage the matrix."
▶ Key Question 4: *What could be done [in each step of the transaction sequence] to exceed our customers' expectations?*

Chapter Nine

Customer Focus Process, Phase Two

THE IMPORTANCE OF FEELING IMPORTANT

Most workers are so seldom given the opportunity to exercise imagination on the job that they will probably be unaware of a phenomenon familiar to seasoned brainstormers: when people feel they've run out of ideas, it usually only means they've run out of *conventional* ideas. If we can inspire them to dig a little deeper, they will tend to move into the less frequently explored regions of their imaginations where repositories of *un*conventional ideas and ways of thinking reside.

The second phase of CFP brainstorming is designed precisely to get participants digging a little deeper. They've looked at each step in the transaction sequence with an eye to exceeding customer expectations; now they revisit each with an eye to making the customer feel important.

Naturally, many of the ideas generated in Phase One would probably already qualify as making the customer feel important—but this doesn't negate the value of Phase Two. We want to avoid missing any opportunity to impress upon our customers a sense that we truly value their business. The emphasis is on how we relate to customers on a *personal* level. Our underlying message becomes: You're not just a dollar sign to us—we see you as a partner and perhaps even a friend. Businesses that have learned to cultivate this kind of bond with their customers usually discover over a period of time that their treatment of customers is echoed in their customers' treatment of them. It's really just basic human dynamics; treat people well, and most will tend to treat you well in return. This is a key element in the strategy to become differentiated from competitors as the better alternative in customers' minds.

The format for Phase Two entails applying the second core principle to each step in the transaction sequence. Note first of all, though, that there will likely be fewer ideas generated per step than was the case the first time around. Indeed, for some steps in the transaction, the group may be unable to come up with a single idea beyond what's already in the matrix. (Phase Two thus typically moves considerably more quickly than Phase One.) This is quite normal for a second pass, and care should be taken to avoid giving the group the impression that they're somehow failing in Phase Two. Instead, it's worth emphasizing to them that this round is purely intended to ensure that no opportunities to make the customer feel important have been overlooked. If few or no ideas are forthcoming, it's probably appropriate to *commend* the group for their thoroughness in Phase One.

Note too that some of the ideas generated in Phase Two may not seem to apply to any one step in particular (as in, Address Customer by Name Whenever Possible). For this reason I recommend creating a new single heading at the extreme right-hand border of the matrix to be entitled General Ideas, as indicated in Matrix Map 5. Throughout Phases Two and Three, ideas that relate to specific steps in the transaction sequence will be posted beneath the relevant step/heading, as in Phase One. Ideas unrelated to any specific step will go under the General Ideas heading.

> **Sandy:** All right, team, we've thought about ways to
> exceed our customers' expectations at every step

MATRIX MAP 5
Heading: General Ideas

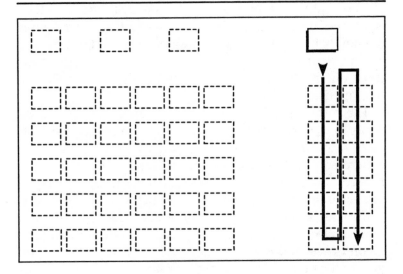

in our transaction sequence, and you've really
come up with some interesting and exciting
ideas. We're now going to look at our second
Customer Focus Principle. It says "Make the
Customer Feel Important." Let's review the
steps in our transaction sequence and see if we
can uncover some additional opportunities to
make the customer feel important. The first step
we identified was, Customer Sees Stand. What
could we do to make customers feel important
when they first see the stand?

▶ *Key Question 5*

*What could be done [in each step of the
transaction sequence] to make the customer feel
important?*

Jerry: A big welcome sign, maybe?

Sandy: Very good, Jerry. Please write that down. Any other ideas?

Larry: It's hard to think of too many for when they just see the stand.

Sandy: True, plus lots of the ideas you've already come up with for this step would make customers feel important, so let's jump to where they approach or we greet them. Any ideas come to mind?

Mary: If we knew something about the customer, it'd be great if we could say something like "I hear you recently bought a new laserdisc machine—how are you enjoying it?" or "How did you make out on your big history exam last week?

Sandy: Okay, that's a great idea, but now how will we summarize that on a Post-it?

Mary: I don't know, how about Show Customer You Know Something about Them if Possible?

Sandy: That's it! Perfect. Please write that down, and I'll put it up under We Greet Customer. Any more for this step?

Sherry: I've got one to go under We Give Customer What Was Ordered: we should always say something like "Hope you enjoy it."

Sandy: Good! Make a note of that, please. Any more ideas for We Greet Customer?

Perry: We should just plain look happy to see them!

Sandy: Absolutely! Please jot that down!

Barry: And no waiting—we greet them right away, even if we can't serve them right away.

Sandy: Yes! That's so important! Write that down, please. What other things could we do to make customers feel important when we first greet them?

As the CFP session progresses, the facilitator can easily fall into the trap of increasingly exhibiting enthusiasm only for the biggest and splashiest innovations, while responding in lukewarm fashion to such "minor" ideas as smiling at customers, being more courteous and pleasant, minimizing delays, etc. Most facilitators embark on their first CFP session feeling that even if it accomplishes no more than getting the team to see the value of smiling at customers more often, it will have been a howling success. Yet they can very quickly become so intoxicated with the group's creative potential for innovative ideas that suddenly something as mundane as merely smiling at customers seems hardly worth getting very excited about anymore.

The danger is that those ideas that appear to have very little impact during the session are typically the least likely to be given serious consideration as worthwhile candidates for implementation later. Yet something as "mundane" as smiling at customers or behaving in a more pleasant manner can have an immeasurably positive effect on customers' perceptions. The fortunes of entire businesses can—and frequently do—turn on factors as mundane as these.

The facilitator must maintain a sense of perspective. The big, splashy ideas may elicit a chorus of appreciative ooohs and aaahs from the group when they're first proposed during the session; yet because of their complexity, cost, or any number of other factors, many of these may never actually become serious contenders for implementation. Cheer your players on, loudly and frequently—but celebrate *all* their ideas, not just the most radical. Sometimes the smallest ideas can ultimately have the biggest effect on the bottom line.

> Sandy: Any more ideas for We Make Change? All right, let's look at our last step, Customer Leaves. How could we make customers feel important when they're leaving our stand?
>
> Gary: We should always make a point of saying something like "We hope you'll come back.
>
> Sandy: Excellent. Make a note of that, please, Gary.

Larry: In fact, maybe to *encourage* them to come back, we could make up some kind of discount coupon for their next visit.

Terry: Hey, yeah, it could say "Next Time, Free Lemonade" or something like that!

Jerry: Here we go again. This guy wants us to go broke!

Sandy: We don't have to work out all the details here and now; the basic idea of some kind of discount to encourage repeat business is just great! It shows our customers we want to see them again.

Mary: We could even have a message printed right on the coupon that says "Please come back—we value your business."

Sandy: Wow! Great ideas! Please get them all written down, and I'll post them here under the General Ideas heading.

When they reach the end of Phase Two, participants may feel they could not possibly come up with any more ideas to improve the customer experience. Yet early in the session we identified expectations that are unique to various categories of customers, and thus far we have done nothing with these customer expectations. That will change in Phase Three.

Snappy Summary

▶ The emphasis in Phase Two is on how we relate to customers on a *personal* level. The way businesses treat their customers is usually echoed in the way customers treat them.

▶ Ideas that do not relate to a specific step in the transaction sequence can be posted under a new General Ideas heading.

▶ Key Question 5: *What could be done [in each step of the transaction sequence] to make the customer feel important?*

Chapter Ten

Customer Focus Process, Phase Three

MAKING FUN OF BUSINESS

"It is a very hard undertaking to seek to please everybody," Publilius Syrus concluded back in the First Century B.C. And let's face it, things haven't really gotten appreciably easier in this regard in the intervening 2,000 years. *Many* undertakings remain as difficult as ever. It is still, for example, a very hard undertaking to seek to cause every arrow fired from one's bow to land in the center of the bull's eye. Or to make every tee shot a hole-in-one. Or to knock down every bowling pin with every try. And yet we continue to try to accomplish these and other equally difficult things—because they're *fun*.

At the end of the baseball season, only two teams are left to battle it out for the World Series. Every ball player in the league now finds himself in one of two groups. Group A includes the players on the teams that made it to the finals; Group B is made up of all the players on all the other teams that didn't. The Group B players are now free to enjoy all the pleasures of early vacation. The Group A players, meanwhile, are working harder than they have all season. They're more exhausted than they've ever been, yet there's more pressure on them to perform than ever before. Everyone is counting on them. Stress levels are at an all-time high; resources are at an all-time low. But which group is having the most fun?

It's a mistake to believe that "fun" must always imply leisure, recreation, loafing. This is the view held by people who find their jobs tedious and demanding and who dream of escape. Others, more fortunate, have discovered that their *work* can be a source of great personal satisfaction and fulfillment. For them, fun often involves working very hard to achieve something very difficult.

As discussed in Chapter 3, any kind of challenging activity can be turned into a game. Pleasing everybody is not only difficult—it's downright impossible. It represents a perfect score, an unattainable goal. The fun can come from striving to achieve this perfect score, observing how close we can get to it, and celebrating every time we get even a little bit closer. When we become more customer-focused, the serious business of business can actually become a source of fun for everyone involved.

In Phase Three of the CFP session we set out to achieve the impossible. We seek to please everybody. We review those expectations that are unique to various categories of customers and try to come up with ways of meeting or even exceeding those expectations in our transaction. Our objective is to find ways to indicate to all of our various categories of customers that we haven't forgotten their special needs or interests, that we haven't left them out, that they're important to us. We want them to feel flattered that we thought of something just for them, that we're tailoring the whole experience to fit their unique requirements. But for them to feel this way, we may need to think about more than just addressing their expectations.

CARING VS. SHOWING WE CARE

Imagine two fast-food restaurant chains competing for the same customer. Both specialize in burgers. Both recognize that their customers are becoming increasingly health and nutrition conscious. Both therefore decide to add leaner low-fat burgers to their menus.

At Burger Heaven, the decision is made to introduce the new product with a minimum of fanfare. Whereas its famous Big Chomper has always been made with meat from Fatso's Meat Factory, the new Yummy Burger, as it's cautiously called, is made with significantly leaner meat supplied by Green Pasture Foods. The plan is to carefully watch how customers respond to the Yummy Burger; if it doesn't catch on it will simply be deleted from the menu as quietly as it was added.

The strategy at Buster Burgers is quite different. It's using a big, glitzy promotional campaign to introduce its new Fat Buster Supreme, "the healthy choice—same great flavor with a fraction of the fat." The printed liners on the food trays depict the new product surrounded by copy extolling the healthful benefits of cutting down on fat consumption.

Which strategy will be most effective? More important, *why*?

The business community's widespread lack of customer focus has conditioned many of us to take for granted that our expectations will be ignored. When they're *not*, we 're inclined to wonder if it was just a fluke. Did they really anticipate my needs and set out to meet them, or was it just some kind of happy accident? People may encounter our efforts to be more customer-focused with out-and-out disbelief. We have to let them know it's not a fluke; we really *are* looking out for them. It may mean not just doing the right things, but also finding ways to let customers *know* we're doing the right things, and that we're doing it for *them*. Both burger chains did what customers wanted—but only one let the customers in on it. Diners at Burger Heaven may *suspect* they're eating a healthier burger, but they won't be certain; they may conclude it's just wishful thinking. They'll eat at Buster Burger instead, because there they know for *sure* they're doing their health a favor.

As we review the various expectations of our various categories of customers, we need to look at them in two ways. First, what could we do to address (or *better* address) this expectation. And second, how can we make this category of customer aware that we're doing this for them? How can we do a better job of *caring* about their needs, and how can we do a better job of *showing* them we care? There's an action component, and there's a communication component. Even if we're doing all the right things, if our customers don't know it, we're not deriving the maximum competitive advantage.

IDEAS THAT ARE FEWER, IDEAS THAT ARE BETTER

Of the three CFP brainstorming phases, the third and final one is loosest and most variable from session to session and group to group. We know right from the outset that it won't be possible to take action related to every expectation for every category of customer. In fact, there may even be contradictory expectations in the matrix. Furthermore, we may already be meeting or exceeding many of the identified expectations. For these reasons, Phase Three may generate fewer ideas than either of the preceding rounds. As was the case with Phase Two, it's important not to give participants the feeling that they're performing poorly if new ideas don't come pouring forth in quite the same profusion as before.

It's not uncommon for ideas that emerge in this round to be among the easiest to implement and yet also be among those with potentially the greatest impact on customers in the particular categories under review. It's here more than anywhere else in the Customer Focus Process that participants are actually focusing on specific customers; ideas generated here will typically be the kind that differentiate businesses most effectively from the competition in their customers' eyes. These will be the little things that make the big difference. It is important for facilitators in this late stage of the session not to greet "little" ideas with little enthusiasm. Scale your appreciation not to the magnitude of the idea but rather to the magnitude of its potential *effect* on customers' perceptions of your business.

One last comment about Phase Three. Some of the ideas generated in this round will relate to a specific step in the transaction sequence and therefore should be posted beneath that particular step in the matrix. Many of the ideas, however, will tend to be more general in nature and will probably be more at home under the General Ideas heading. Whenever there's even the slightest doubt in your mind about where a given idea should be posted, waste no time worrying about the matter; stick it under General Ideas and move on to the next one.

> **Sandy:** Well, team, you've thought of ideas to exceed customer expectations every step of the way, and you've come up with some great ideas to make customers feel important. Our third Customer Focus Principle says "Tailor the Experience to Fit the Customer." We'll look for ways to do this by reviewing the specific expectations for the different customer categories we identified earlier and posted over here, at the beginning of the matrix. Our first customer category is Construction Workers. We said one of the things they expect is Fast Service because their breaks aren't long. So—what could we do to give them faster service?

▶ *KEY QUESTION 6A (ACTION-RELATED):*
_____

What could be done [to address this particular expectation for this particular category of customer]?

Perry: The big bottleneck is always when they pay us. They're fumbling for the coins in their pockets, and they have to wait for us to give them their change—that's when the big lines form. What if we just sold bunches of tickets to the foreman ahead of time, and the workers just handed us a ticket when we handed them their drinks? No counting, no change—that's got to speed things up.

Sandy: Wow, Perry, that's fantastic! Please get that down on a Post-it! Those construction workers will really appreciate this. Now, how can we make sure they know we're doing it just for them?

▶ KEY QUESTION 6B (COMMUNICATION-RELATED):

What could be done to ensure [this particular customer category] recognizes we're [addressing this particular expectation] with them in mind?

Perry: We could get something printed right on the tickets—the name of their construction company, maybe, and something about "to give you more time to enjoy your break" or something along those lines.

Sandy: That's perfect! Please get that down on a Post-it as well—I'll put them here under General Ideas. What else could we do to speed things up for our construction workers?

Sherry: I was thinking we could maybe have pre-filled cups of lemonade set aside before their breaks; they wouldn't even have to wait for us to fill cups.

Sandy: Another great idea! How will we let them know these pre-filled cups are for them—any thoughts on that?

Larry: Sherry's idea got me thinking, what if we filled a big cooler with crushed ice? The next expectation we identified for them was Lots of Ice; we could wedge their pre-filled cups into this big mound of ice and then maybe put a sign on the cooler with their company logo on it.

Sandy: Fabulous! Two birds with one stone! Please get all this down.

Sherry: The pre-filled cups should also be *big* cups because the next expectation we put down for them was Big Portions.

Sandy: *Three* birds with one stone! Now Sherry, how can we let them know those big cups are there because we know they have a big thirst?

Sherry: Maybe that's exactly what we should tell them. The sign on the cooler could say something like "Construction-Size Portions for Your Con-struction-Size Thirst."

Sandy: These are great ideas! Please pass me your Post-its; I want to make sure we have everything written down. We've got Pre-filled Large-portion Cups, Cooler Full of Crushed Ice, Large Cups Chilled Prior to A.M & P.M. Breaks, and Sign on Cooler: Logo and Reference to Construction-size Thirst. Is that everything?

Jerry: That's everything.

Sandy: Great. And I see here there's one idea we put up earlier. Perry, I think it was suggested we deliver drinks right to the workers at their site. That too is a pretty exciting possibility, so I'm going to add that note to the others I'm posting under General Ideas.

It is typical of the CFP's third and final brainstorming phase to keep the facilitator bouncing back and forth from one end of the matrix to the other, from Expectations on the far left to General Ideas on the far right. Indeed, depending on the ingenuity of the group, the final General Ideas heading may end up presiding over considerably more than just two columns of ideas.

Once all expectations for all categories of customers have been considered and all ideas posted, the group's creative work is complete, and the session is near its conclusion. What remains is to give participants the opportunity to take action on some of their ideas. What remains, in other words, is to transform customer-focus from a concept to a reality.

Snappy Summary

- ▶ Pleasing everybody is impossible. Yet striving to achieve this impossible goal can make the serious business of business a source of fun for everyone involved.
- ▶ We must do the right things for customers, but we must also show them we're doing it for them. There's an *action* component, and there's a *communication* component.
- ▶ Key Question 6A (action-related): *What could be done [to address this particular expectation for this particular category of customer]?*
- ▶ Key Question 6B (communication-related): *What could be done to ensure [this particular customer category] recognizes we're [addressing this particular expectation] with them in mind?*

Chapter Eleven

Transforming Ideas into Actions

BOBO AND THE CHEESE

A television station where I worked decades ago was patrolled during the night by a crackerjack security guard named Bobo. Usually Bobo was accompanied on his rounds by his human assistant, John—but not always. Bobo was perfectly capable of doing his job on his own if John requested it. And woe to any prowlers. Bobo was one of those German shepherds that looked more like a wolf than a dog, and he could behave more like one too if the situation warranted it.

But this was also an uncommonly gentle and obedient animal. John enjoyed demonstrating this by placing a piece of cheese atop Bobo's snout. The dog had a passion for cheese but would not budge until John gave him the go-ahead. The cheese would remain on Bobo's snout, untouched, for minutes on end. The dog's expression was so calm and matter-of-fact that you began to wonder whether he even realized there was any cheese there at all. John would pretend to forget all about it and busy himself with some trivial task nearby. There was nothing to suggest that the dog was experiencing any sense of anticipation whatsoever. He just stared blankly at his master, apparently prepared to wait for hours if necessary. Without even turning to look at the dog, John would raise an index finger and give it a quick, tiny spin in the air. You'd hear the canine jaws snap shut before you had time to turn and see Bobo fling the cheese in the air with a toss of his massive head and catch it between his teeth. It was down the hatch and gone in a split-second blur. This dog *loved* cheese.

When facilitators reach the end of their first CFP session, they may find themselves feeling a little like Bobo must have felt with the cheese perched on his snout. Here's this matrix loaded with exciting, compelling ideas the facilitator is *dying* to see implemented, and yet he or she is now expected to exhibit a perfectly calm and matter-of-fact demeanor while participants take their sweet time deciding whether they will or won't take any sort of action on this or that idea. It can be torture.

Everybody knows that Gladys, the receptionist, often loses track of the time of day and sweetly answers a caller's 4:30 p.m. request to speak to Ms. Finkle with, "Just a moment, I'll see if she's come back from lunch yet." Everybody knows a lot of customers are being given the impression that the whole staff routinely takes four- and five-hour lunch breaks. Someone has contributed an idea to the matrix that reads Big Digital Clock Right beside Main Switchboard. And now, at the end of the session, as participants review the posted ideas for possible action items, you stand there gazing hopefully at Gladys, and turning your gaze to the "clock-beside-switchboard" Post-it, and turning back to Gladys, thinking, Come on, Gladys, this one's for you, go for it, I'll even pay for the darn clock, for cryin' out loud! But all Gladys seems interested in doing is watching all the other participants as *they* review the matrix, and smiling at them in her kindly way, as if she feels that none of this could possibly apply to her, but it's certainly interesting to watch all these other, more creative people as they try to decide what they're going to undertake to do. It can truly be torture.

Back to Bobo and cheese for a moment. Can a dog—even a very intelligent dog—think strategically? It was almost as if this dog had developed a strategy for increasing the total amount of cheese that came his way. It was as if he realized that the more impressively he ignored the cheese until John gave the signal, the greater was John's incentive to use this particular trick to demonstrate his superior dog-training skills—which meant more opportunities to eat cheese. In effect, the more convincingly indifferent to cheese Bobo appeared, the more cheese Bobo got to enjoy. (Which raises some intriguing questions about just precisely who was training whom in this whole operation.)

There's a useful lesson for CFP facilitators here. The more convincingly you can make your group feel that they are under *no obligation* to implement *anything* in the matrix, the greater your chances of having them volunteer to take action on some of the posted ideas. And the easiest way for facilitators to put participants at ease in this regard is to actually be prepared to consider the session a success *even if not a single action initiative is taken at its conclusion.*

The mere fact that the matrix is full of ideas for making your business more customer-focused means you have already succeeded in getting a group of workers thinking about ways to delight customers. You've given your people *awareness*, the vital first step toward a change in behavior. They know now what customer focus would look like in their workplace. They can easily imagine the difference it would make for their customers and for themselves. Back on the job they'll start seeing with new eyes instances where customer expectations are *not* being exceeded or where customers are *not* being made to feel important. Even if they don't feel quite ready to take action immediately, you have certainly gotten them thinking about their customers. Many elaborate (and expensive) two- or three-day corporate seminars set out to do no more than this and succeed only marginally.

CFP facilitators should reach the end of the session feeling that even if no immediate action commitments are made as a result of the brainstorming, the participants have never-theless been through an extremely valuable educational experience—one which beautifully sets the stage for *future* customer-focus activities. The session may conclude with no one actually making a decision to take responsibility for acquiring a clock for the switchboard area, yet someone did come up with that very good idea. And the next time Gladys treats the gang to a batch of her superb home-made butter tarts, it may seem perfectly appropriate to express collective appreciation with a small gift of some sort—like, say, a clock for her work area. If facilitators can recognize that simply generating a bunch of good *ideas* for becoming more cus-tomer focused represents a fairly significant positive achieve-ment in its own right, they will experience little or no anguish at the end of the session even if no immediate action com-mitments are made. And like Bobo, who gets to eat more cheese by appearing more indifferent to cheese, facilitators who create no pressure to take action usually wind up with more actions being taken.

PLEASE FEEL FREE TO VOLUNTEER IMMEDIATELY—OR ELSE

The end of the session can present a challenge for partici-pants as well. When the fun and magic of creative brain-storming come to an end, the group can sometimes experience a feeling like waking from a pleasant dream. Suddenly they're back in the real world, where they must soon once again face real customers with real problems. Suddenly the items in the matrix may begin to look like extra work, activities that would require an outlay of more time and more energy than they have to spare. Suddenly they may find themselves looking at the facilitator with a silent gaze that wordlessly asks, You're not actually expect-ing us to *do* any of this stuff, are you?

This is a critical moment. They're wondering if their ideas are now going to be used against them. Was this whole CFP session just the leader's way of sugar-coating the bitter message—that their treatment of customers has somehow been deficient all along and that they'd better shape up right now or else? If they're given even the slightest reason to believe that this was all just a sneaky way of getting them to do things they normally wouldn't be inclined to do, there will probably be a general crossing of the arms and digging in of the heels in preparation for battle.

The facilitator's top priority at this critical moment is to reassure the participants that they're not going to be urged, coaxed, cajoled, or tricked into doing anything they don't want to do. As was outlined in the opening remarks at the beginning of the session, the basic purpose of the whole exercise is to generate ideas for developing a competitive advantage by improving the customer experience, and this they have accomplished admirably. Thanks to their creativity, the session was a great success. They will now be allowed to review the contents of the matrix in case there might be one or more action items they'd *like* to take on—but this decision will be entirely their own, and no one will be punished in any way whatsoever for failing to make an action commitment. Only time will tell what, if anything, will come of most of these ideas.

THE ACTION LOG

In most cases there will be some participants who *will* volunteer to take some action initiatives. Some ideas in the matrix will seem so sensible and easy to implement, for example, that there wouldn't be any good reason *not* to take them on. Some will clearly serve to *reduce* work, not create more, or to make things more pleasant for the *worker* as well as for the customer. Some ideas, even fairly elaborate ones, may have elicited a spontaneous chorus of appreciative ooohs and aaahs when first proposed during the brainstorming. The gratified originators of these crowd-pleaser ideas typically feel a strong sense of personal identification with their ideas and will often volunteer to implement them in the hope of inspiring similarly positive reactions in customers.

Whatever the reason for doing so, whenever a participant volunteers to take on an action item, you need to record the fact in a CFP Action Log of some kind. Much of Chapter 3 discussed the importance of making work feel like play, of cheering the players on, of making the players feel like winners. This Action Log becomes a perfect mechanism to permit you to do this, as described in greater detail in the next chapter. At its simplest, the log may be no more than a sheet of ring-binder paper divided into five columns: *Action, Person, Target Completion Date, Actual Completion Date,* and *Notes.*

The first column records what precisely will be done. The wording here may need to be more precise and detailed than appears on the corresponding Post-it note in the matrix. For instance, the idea of providing thirsty construction workers with big portions of lemonade was recorded as Big Portions in the matrix. This may translate into "Will check with cup suppliers for availability and pricing of larger-size cups" in the Action Log. Prompt Service, if selected by a sales clerk, may become "Will always give a customer on the premises priority attention over all other considerations." For a receptionist wanting to take on an action item related to the same Prompt Service idea, the Action Log entry may become "Will always strive to answer the phone before the third ring."

As with the wording of the original Post-its, it's advisable to use the participants' own words as much as possible to describe the specifics of the action they intend to take. Occasionally, however, it may be necessary to help them distinguish between an *action* and an *objective.* An action can be thought of as an activity someone could take a photo of someone else doing. Whereas "Will be more courteous when dealing with customers" is truly a commendable objective, it doesn't specify what will be done to *achieve* the objective. The facilitator would need to ask, "How, in what way?" Responses such as "Will maintain friendly eye contact whenever customers are speaking to me" or "When walking to another part of the store with a customer, will always hold doors or gates open for him or her" represent more clearly defined actions. "Better internal communication," "more teamwork," and "greater sensitivity to customer needs" are all excellent objectives but are difficult to measure or quantify. "Publish an internal newsletter," "hold weekly interdepartmental problem-solving meetings," and "survey our customers to determine how well we meet their needs" are all actions.

The second column identifies who is taking on a particular action item. In most cases, a single name will appear. Occasionally more than one individual will want to pursue a given activity. There may even be the odd case when *everyone* wants to tackle one specific idea. This kind of duplication should be very actively encouraged; it builds teamwork and helps ensure that customers are treated similarly by different workers. It is extremely important to record the names of every individual who is making a commitment to action even if (*especially* if) the list is long. Effective follow-up to the CFP session will be impossible unless the Action Log is accurate and complete.

In the Target Completion Date column, record the date on which the participants estimate their action item will be completed—or, if it's to be an ongoing activity, when it will begin. This information is solely for the purpose of making it easier for you to follow up at an appropriate time with a request for a progress report. Participants should not be made to feel that their voluntary activities suddenly have a rigid deadline attached to them.

The fourth column, Actual Completion Date, is where the log will record which actions were actually taken to delight customers, and when. This is the specific information that gives us such perfect opportunities to delight our own internal customers, our employees.

The last column, Notes, is reserved for any additional information or commentary related to the specific action items listed. If a worker were unable to complete the action due to illness or some other factor beyond his or her control, for example, it may be worth making a note to that effect to guard against a faulty memory leading to an erroneous conclusion that the worker lost interest in the project. Or if implementation of an idea turned out to be more challenging than anyone foresaw, and yet the worker(s) persevered and successfully got it done, this may be deserving of special recognition, and a written reminder in the Notes column will ensure that such dedication will not be accidentally overlooked.

A growing number of business leaders are discovering the morale-building power of recognizing the efforts and good work of their workers on a regular basis. The challenge for these managers revolves around how to stay in the know about what their employees are actually up to on behalf of customers. The CFP Action Log represents a simple but highly effective means of documenting workers' customer-related activities.

WATCH WHAT YOU SAY—I'M WRITING ALL THIS DOWN

It's not inconceivable that participants will wonder exactly why you're writing all their commitments down on paper. Is this so you'll have a written record of all those who *didn't* take on any action items? Is this going to affect my next raise, my next performance evaluation? Does this mean if I volunteer to do something I can expect some kind of bonus or something? What's the deal?

My recommendation is that you make it clear that your intention is to follow up at a later date to discover which ideas did or didn't work and why. *Your sole objective is to help make the business more customer-focused.* The follow-up will give you a better picture of how well the group's efforts to make the business more customer-focused are working. If there are significant successes, it may mean further CFP sessions would be appropriate at some point. The Action Log may identify worthy recipients of some form of nonmonetary recognition, but under no circumstances should it be used punitively.

The basic function of the Action Log, in short, is not to evaluate how well the participants performed during or after the CFP session; its real purpose is to assess how well the CFP session *itself* worked in terms of making the business more customer-focused. Obviously the easiest way to judge the session's effectiveness is to track any customer-focus activities initiated as a direct result of the session. A written record is necessary to do this effectively. (But even if no initiatives are taken in the session proper and the Action Log thus remains blank, it's by no means inconceivable that some workers may unofficially undertake to do some things differently as a result of awareness gained in the session. This too would be a measure of success for the session.)

> Sandy: Were there any more ideas about how we might tailor the experience of coming to our lemonade stand to this last category of customer? All right, well, we've now done some brainstorming around all three of our Customer Focus Principles, and if we take a look at the whole matrix, it's easy to see you've certainly come up

with a lot of terrific ideas for drawing customers away from our competitors. I'd now like to give you an opportunity to review the ideas you've come up with in case any of you would like to take one or more on as personal action items. Please take as long as you wish to review the ideas posted in the matrix.

Gary: So the idea is we each have to take one on, is that it?

Sandy: Actually you don't *have* to take any action items on at all if you don't feel like it. You're free to take on none at all, or one, or as many as you like.

Perry: Well okay, I think I'd like to look into this idea, Put up Colorful Streamers Like in Car Lot. My dad works at a car lot, and I think we can get some streamers for free.

Sandy: Great! Let me just make a note of this. Should I just put down "will check availability of color streamers"?

Perry: Um, yeah, sure, that's fine, except I have a question. Since you're writing this down, let's say one of us agrees to take on an action item, but then for some reason it doesn't work out, does that mean—?

Sandy: All it means is that something got in your way. We'll then put our heads together and see if there's some way around the problem. If not, we'll see if there's an alternate action idea you might enjoy pursuing instead.

Perry: So the fact that you're writing it down doesn't mean we're going to be in some kind of trouble if things don't work out?

Sandy: Definitely not. I'm only writing it down so I won't risk forgetting to follow up with you about it later. If it turns out that you can't get the streamers for free, we may want to proceed to plan B and see about buying some.

Perry: Okay, well, I can ask my dad about that over the weekend.

Sandy: So under Target Completion Date I can put Monday's date?

Perry: Sure.

Sandy: Great. There's one action commitment already. Anybody else want to take one on?

Larry: This Discount Coupons for Next Visit idea—how about I talk to a printer about getting some made up?

Sandy: Perfect. I'll put down "will meet with printer about discount coupons" and then your name. When do you think you could have that completed, Larry?

Larry: I guess maybe before the end of the month.

Sandy: Fine. I'll put down the first of next month as the target completion date.

Gary: I'm going to start doing this Round off Change in Customer's Favor.

Sherry: Oh rats—I was going to volunteer to do that one!

Sandy: That's okay, you can both take on the same action item; there's no problem there.

Sherry: Okay, but I'd also like to make up some "happy music" tapes for my boombox, give customers a little atmosphere.

Sandy: That's fine—two of you round off change, and Sherry provides happy music.

Barry: *Three* of us round off change; I'd like to take that one on too.

Mary: Me too, actually.

Terry: Maybe we should all take it on.

Sandy: How do the rest of you feel? Everybody want to
take this on?

Jerry: Sure, why not?

Sandy: That's great! All right, let me get all this down.
You know, people, we're going to absolutely
clobber the competition!

The Action Log sends a subtle but powerful message to the
group—one that is probably better left unspoken, one that
has the greatest impact on workers if they are able to discern
it for themselves. This session, your careful notations into
the log imply, was not a one-shot, flash-in-the-pan event
that your leader intends to forget all about in a day and a
half. There will be follow-up. There will be further discussion of these issues. There will be celebration, if warranted
by successes achieved; if not, there will be other approaches
and techniques pursued. Our pressing need to become more
customer-focused does not disappear just because this particular method may not prove to be the best way to get us
there. Ultimately we will achieve our customer-focus objectives, one way or another, using a voluntary system like CFP
or some other system if need be. We *will* become the better
alternative. We *will* become the winning team. We have no
choice. Our very survival depends on it.

Snappy Summary

▶ The more convincingly you can make your
group feel that they are under no obligation to
implement anything in the matrix, the greater
your chances of having them volunteer to take
action on some of the posted ideas.

▶ Even if no action commitments are made at
the end of the session, the participants have
nevertheless been through an extremely

valuable educational experience which beautifully sets the stage for future customer-focus activities.

▶ The CFP Action Log should be divided into five columns: Action, Person, Target Completion Date, Actual Completion Date, and Notes.

▶ The basic function of the Action Log is not to evaluate how well the participants performed during or after the CFP session—its real purpose is to assess how well the session itself worked in terms of making the business more customer-focused.

Chapter Twelve

Maintaining Customer Focus

DANGER AHEAD

"A little learning," warned Alexander Pope, "is a dang'rous thing." Business leaders who set out to cultivate among workers a greater awareness of the nature and power of customer focus may discover that hidden among the many major blessings that ensue is a minor curse. To a child with a hammer in his hand, the old saying goes, everything starts looking like a nail. Workers armed with an understanding of what customer focus looks and feels like will begin seeing its presence or absence in their various daily dealings with all and sundry. This is the good news—they've become sensitized to the whole customer focus issue and will be especially watchful for lapses in their own workplace. The bad news is that they will therefore be especially watchful for lapses in their *leaders*. It means if you're going to equip your team with an ability to spot customer focus deficiencies at a glance, you'll want to make sure they don't all end up pointing at you as a particularly appalling example.

"If a little knowledge is dangerous," wrote Thomas Huxley a century and a half after Pope, "where is the man who has so much as to be out of danger?" Far more dangerous than a little knowledge is no knowledge at all. The way to avoid the danger of being held up as an example of bad behavior is *not* to keep everybody in the dark about what constitutes bad behavior, but rather to begin exhibiting *good* behavior.

The Customer Focus Process produces two distinct outputs: a matrix of brainstormed ideas and an Action Log. The information contained in the matrix can be applied in answering the workers' question, "What could we do to improve the total customer experience?" The information contained in the Action Log can similarly be applied in answering the leader's question, "What could I use as the basis for celebration, for recognition, for motivating my team, for making them feel like winners, for making work feel like play—in short, for improving the total *internal* customer experience?" Here, therefore, is the perfect opportunity to begin exhibiting what the workers will now be equipped to recognize as good behavior. It would be a dangerous thing indeed to exhort our workers to abandon old behaviors and adopt new ones while we ourselves blithely go on doing the very sorts of things we've helped them recognize as totally inappropriate. So in this final chapter we'll look at how to help the team get the most out of their CFP output, the matrix, and how we can get the most out of ours, the Action Log.

AFTER THE SESSION

Whether there will be only one CFP session ever or dozens over a period of years, it's always advisable to keep a given matrix up and on display at least until a follow-up meeting related to that particular session can be held.

Experience with CFP has shown that session participants will tend to casually revisit a prominently posted matrix from time to time just to take another look. This can sometimes lead to a quiet, unannounced decision to implement one of the ideas listed there. It can also encourage workers to add to the matrix a creative idea or two that has come to them hours or days after the session has concluded.

A tidy, orderly matrix invites this kind of postsession inspection. In the hurly-burly of brainstorming, ideas may have been hastily posted in a somewhat disorderly fashion in the matrix. Also, hurried penmanship may have made some ideas difficult to read. And some ideas that were perfectly clear when posted may afterwards become quite puzzling. For instance, days after the session it may be difficult even for the originator of the idea to recall what Rent Them unless the Other One Can Do Both was actually referring to. For all of these reasons, it may be a good idea to "dress the matrix" after the session.

Dressing the matrix can involve repositioning ideas neatly and in the appropriate places, eliminating duplicate ideas, adding words or phrases where necessary for clarity (Rent *Clown Costumes* unless the Other *Vendor* Can *Repair and Resize*), and even rewriting some ideas altogether where the original is illegible—though in this last case it's advantageous to have the originator of the idea do the rewrite in his or her own hand, if possible. A neater, more legible matrix attracts more casual perusal and therefore more potential activity.

THE ALL-IMPORTANT FOLLOW-UP MEETING

In swinging a golf club as in managing a business, follow-through is everything. Every CFP session in which two or more participants volunteered to take on action items requires a follow-up meeting, whether another full-blown CFP session is to be held later or not. The meeting has specific objectives (outlined below); but it also serves to reinforce the perception that though the CFP session may be behind us, we're not all going to simply forget all about this whole customer focus idea and revert to business as usual. On the contrary, an emphasis on improving the customer experience is actually going to increasingly *become* our usual way of doing business.

1. **Format for follow-up meeting if no participants took on action items in the CFP session**

   None. In this (rare) case, there's no point in holding a general follow-up meeting. Instead, it might be worth asking the team how they would feel about participating in a second CFP session at some future date. If there appears to be interest, you may encounter less reluctance to voluntarily take on action items after this second session. (Suggestions for additional sessions appear below.) If the team expresses little or no interest in any further Customer Focus activities, it may mean it's time for you to begin doing some hard thinking about the future of your business and the kinds of training or educational material you may need to consider investing in for your team.

2. **Format for follow-up meeting if only one participant took on one or more action items in the CFP session**

   None. In this (equally rare) case, there's once again no point in holding a general follow-up meeting. Instead, deal with the noble volunteer on a one-on-one basis. If the action item was not successfully implemented, commend the individual for at least giving it a try. If the attempt was successful, provide ample appropriate recognition. As in the previous case, it's probably worthwhile to investigate the team's willingness to participate in a second CFP session later.

3. **Format for follow-up meeting if more than one participant took on one or more action items in the CFP session**

   This more typical scenario calls for a follow-up meeting. Even if only two participants took the plunge, the rest of the team should be given the chance to observe first-hand what will ensue. This meeting may last anywhere from 10 minutes or so (if only a few action items need to be discussed) to several hours (if there are a slew of action items to review). Regardless of its duration, the meeting's primary objectives are the same.

Primary Objectives of Follow-up Meeting

- Allow participants to relate in their own words what their activity entailed, problems encountered along the way, how problems were overcome, successes, benefits to customers, benefits to themselves, etc.
- (If implementation was unsuccessful): Allow other members of the team to brainstorm ways around the problem or obstacle—including volunteering to become involved, if appropriate.
- (If implementation was successful): Record details of the success under the Notes column in the Action Log.
- Invite any and all participants to voluntarily take on additional action items from the existing matrix; (record these commitments in the Action Log).
- Invite participants to add to the matrix any new ideas which may have come to mind since the CFP session.
- Celebrate successes with an appropriate level of fanfare and fun.

That last point may be the most important objective of all; more about celebration and recognition a little later. In some cases it may be appropriate to incorporate a follow-up meeting into the introduction of a subsequent CFP session proper. In this case, simply conclude the follow-up meeting normally and then, as Opening Remarks to the new session, clarify which Transaction Sequence will be analyzed this time around and proceed to identify Steps in the Transaction Sequence.

CFP SESSIONS IN SUCCESSION

For many smaller businesses—particularly those with simple, straightforward customer transactions that vary little from day to day—a single CFP session can go a long way. Still, it may only be a matter of time before another session will seem appropriate. If there has been significant staff turnover since the first session, for example, it would probably be a good idea to help the new employees experience for themselves how a customer-focused approach can improve their worklives. Also, if the competitive pressure continues to grow (as it's bound to do, even if only because your competitors are stealing your customer-focus innovations and are merely duplicating them), a fresh arsenal of innovations may be needed to put some more distance between your business and the rest of the pack. And, of course, subsequent sessions act as re-energizers, helping to keep workers' attention focused on customers.

In larger, more complex kinds of organizations, where customer transactions take many forms, it becomes advantageous to devote separate CFP sessions to each of the key types of customer transactions. This may involve separate workteams, some of which may need to participate in multiple sessions. It may also involve sessions that focus on transactions where the customers happen to be *internal*.

Before the magnitude of the undertaking begins to over-whelm, let me emphasize that there is no virtue in crowding CFP sessions close together in time. My rule of thumb is that no one team should participate in sessions that are less than one month apart and that in fact two months between sessions is even better. If sessions are strung too closely to-gether, the brainstorming activity itself tends to lose some of its electricity and can become somewhat stale. It also means there is insufficient time for action items to affect enough customers to allow for an accurate assessment of effectiveness. Spreading the sessions out over an extended period of time makes the deployment of CFP more manage-able, it minimizes the danger of facilitator burnout, and it keeps the brainstorming activity fresh and lively, maximiz-ing its motivational effect for facilitator and participants alike.

WHO SHOULD LEAD MULTIPLE SESSIONS?

If there are to be separate teams of workers participating in CFP sessions, it is highly advisable that the functional leader of each team be the facilitator for his or her team's session. The exception would be where the functional leader of a given team is so desperately lacking in facilitation skills that as an employee motivator the session would likely do more harm than good. In this case the next best option is that a skilled facilitator *other than the CEO or senior executive* lead the session for this particular team. Why not the top dog? Two reasons.

First, if the senior person typically has little direct contact with the team members on a day-to-day basis but then shows up to personally lead the session, his or her involve-ment may drive participants' apprehension levels to un-precedented heights: "We must *really* be in trouble around here! No way I'm going to open *my* mouth!" Second, he or she has a much more important role to play in CFP—namely, to teach the other facilitators how to lead sessions!

There is no better way for leaders of larger organizations to demonstrate their commitment to developing greater customer focus than by personally instructing team leaders and/or group facilitators on how best to lead workers through the CFP experience. It makes crystal clear both their thorough understanding of the process and their high expectations in terms of results—a big motivator for the facilitators!

LEADING A *HOW TO LEAD A SESSION* SESSION

Once you understand the elements of the process, you can teach someone else the fundamentals easily and quickly (I've done it in half an hour over the telephone). The most effective technique, though, is to put your facilitators-to-be through a mock session in which they're the participants. To keep their attention on the structure of the process and avoid having them get lost in actual brainstorming for their business, it's critical that you get them to pretend *they're a work team in an imaginary firm that has as little in common with your actual business as possible*. Simple businesses with simple transaction are best for learning the process—a lemonade stand, a shoe shine stand, a car wash. Once they've experienced all phases of the process from the participants' point of view (which, in the context of an imaginary business, shouldn't take much more than an hour or so), you should then walk them through a detailed review of all the phases and steps you put them through, with particular emphasis on the following key elements:

- Use of different colors of Post-it notes (and/or ink)
- Procedure for transferring ideas to the matrix
- Matrix layout

- Opening Remarks
- Use of Key Questions to prompt brainstorming
- Three Customer Focus Principles
- Use of the Action Log
- How to recognize and celebrate successes

Your facilitators will also require some guidance regarding how to conduct follow-up meetings; a simple walk-through of the format should be sufficient. The importance of the celebration aspect cannot be overemphasized. And to the extent that their participants do end up achieving successes worth celebrating, so must you in turn recognize and celebrate *their* successes. But how do you make recognition and celebration key components of the whole Customer Focus initiative?

CELEBRATING CUSTOMER FOCUS SUCCESSES

In the film industry, it's become customary to promote new movies by releasing a "The Making of . . ." documentary to television. Even before they've bought their tickets, the potential audience is shown all the trickery and deception that were used to achieve the movie's illusions. Yet rather than diminishing the film's appeal, this approach has a proven track record for drawing larger numbers into the theaters. And professional magicians know that other magicians usually make the most appreciative audiences, even though they often know "how it's done." Understanding the mechanics of how an effect is achieved or an objective accomplished, it seems, can actually serve to heighten appreciation.

This is good for CFP facilitators to know because their goal in celebrating the successes of their participants is to bring the same Wow Factor into play that the participants used to delight their customers. The recipients of such recognition may realize that what they're getting represents a clear application of one or another of the Customer Focus Principles, but this awareness will do nothing to diminish the impact of the experience and may well even heighten it.

Facilitators can sometimes find it a little frustrating, during group brainstorming activities in the CFP session, to have to refrain from blurting out their own imaginative ideas and instead patiently prompt the participants. Well, you *will* have a chance to show your stuff to the group after all. Your opportunity comes in the follow-up meeting(s). You see, *prior* to the follow-up meeting you're going to engage in a little CFP brainstorming yourself.

Find a time and a place to conduct your top-secret solitary CFP session where you're not likely to be caught in the act by anyone on your team; you want the element of surprise working for you. You'll be creating two mini-matrices. The customers, in this case, are your participants, so you begin by creating a matrix heading for each member of the team. Under each, instead of expectations, list as many hobbies or special interests as you can for that particular individual. Include favorite sports teams, preferred types of music, favorite local restaurants—anything and everything you can think of. (If you know little or nothing about one or more members of the team, you'll need to do some research. Make it discreet; you don't want to arouse suspicions among workers or their friends and relatives. Concentrate initially on those workers who volunteered to take on action items during the CFP session.)

Now create a duplicate set of headings, once again bearing the names of the team members. It is in this second matrix area that you can give your creativity free rein; here you'll capture ideas for suitable "prizes" for the various participants. You're looking for ways to recognize achievement and celebrate success but in ways that apply the three

Customer Focus Principles: you want to exceed their expectations, make them feel important, and tailor the recognition
to fit their particular interests. The intent here is to *recognize*,
not to *reward*. You're simply acknowledging good work and
using positive reinforcement to encourage more of the same.
These should not, therefore, be lavish, elaborate, expensive
items. They're intended to be simple mementos of appreciation, personalized keepsakes, souvenirs with sentimental
rather than monetary value. The emphasis should be on fun,
on laughter, on celebration. The handing over of these items
should give the follow-up meeting something of the flavor
of an informal, spontaneous party.

Examples: Terry enjoys collecting and flying kites. For
successfully implementing his "happy hour for primary-
school kids" idea at the lemonade stand, he's presented with
a fancy kite inscribed with the words, "For helping make
our younger customers' satisfaction levels soar, may you
enjoy many happy hours making this soar as well." Mary
is just learning to sew her own clothes; she also recently
acquired a new puppy. Her action item involved simply
making an effort to smile at customers more often. A number of possibilities: get a photo of her smiling and present
her with a copy inscribed, "The smile that keeps customers
coming back." Or present her with a book of sewing patterns along with a bookmark inscribed, "Hoping some of
these sewing projects will keep you smiling." Or give her
a doggie bowl with a card that reads, "In recognition of the
smile that 'bowls' our customers over."

You get the idea. You may think up four "doggie" ideas
for Mary, and two "sewing" ideas, and a couple more "smile-
related" ideas—get them all up in the matrix, because Mary
may take on more action items in the near future and be
deserving of further recognition. Your creative challenge is
to find some way to "theme" the item to the recipient's
action item, or special interest, or both. It won't always be
easy, but it's the very same sort of challenge participants

face in the CFP session when you keep asking, "What *else* could we do to exceed this customer's expectations?" The more ingeniously you manage to surprise and delight them, the more you inspire them to try to top you. Show them what you can do. Show them how even when it may look like there couldn't possibly be any more good ideas that haven't already been thought of and done, there's still more, there's always more.

REWARDING CUSTOMER FOCUS SUCCESSES

It's important to keep all recognition associated with CFP successes *nonmonetary* in nature. Almost as destructive to the process as the fear of dire consequences for failing to take action initiatives is the opposite anticipation of big-buck rewards for doing so. Workers need to discover for themselves that the primary rewards to be derived from becoming more customer-focused revolve around such issues as greater job satisfaction, more recognition from happy internal and external customers, less frustration and aggravation in the workplace, greater job security and opportunities for advancement, the sense of pride associated with being a winning player on a winning team. Cash awards, which allow workers to begin attaching specific dollar figures to various kinds of actions or activities, can only lead to frustration and resentment. ("You mean to tell me they gave you a hundred smackers just for agreeing to *smile* more often? Hell, I said I'd be more *polite*, which you and I both know means doing a lot more than just smiling, and all I got was a crummy seventy-five bucks! What a ripoff!") Employees will start volunteering to do those things to which they figure the most dollars will be attached. The result: they're not more customer-focused, they're more *dollar*-focused. And to make matters worse, it's not customer dollars they're going after, it's *your* dollars. Not good.

Naturally it will be appropriate to reward consistently customer-focused workers with better-paying assignments, with promotions and raises, perhaps even with special cash bonuses. But it should be clear to the recipient and to his or her peers that these monies are a reflection of a *high overall level of customer focus* for which you have many examples— they are not based on one or two isolated activities to which everyone can now easily attach a dollar value. In short, *recognize* individual isolated instances of customer-focused behavior, and *reward* consistent ongoing patterns of customer-focused behavior.

Your long-tem role in the Customer Focus Process becomes that of cheerleader. Recognize and celebrate your workers' successes at every opportunity because doing so makes them feel like winners. It makes being a part of your business feel like being part of the winning team. It makes everyone want to work even harder at luring customers away from the competition. It fuels continued application of the Customer Focus Principles. It makes working for a living *fun* again. And, equally desirable, it makes your business more profitable.

FOCUSING ON FOCUS GROUPS

In Chapter 4 we discussed the notion of informally "hiring" customers as free consultants. The Customer Focus Process provides a means for taking this concept considerably further. After one or more CFP sessions have taken place, a great deal can be gained by inviting a representative group of customers to participate in a formal focus group discussion. The key objectives of such a meeting then become:

1. To validate the workteam's assumptions about customers' expectations.

2. To validate the workteam's assumptions about the steps that make up the Transaction Sequence.
3. To solicit creative ideas for improving the customer experience from customers themselves.

Ideally, the team members who participated in the original CFP session(s) should also be a part of any subsequent focus group meetings, even if their role this time around becomes more that of observers. If this level of participation isn't easily arranged, an effort should be made to have at the very least *one* representative of the team present to observe and report back to the others. The original CFP matrix needs to be posted where the customers can see it and read its contents. Provide each customer with a pad of Post-it notes (preferably of a color not yet present in the matrix) and a marker.

In terms of format, begin with Opening Remarks that explain to the group how the CFP session was conducted and what you hope to accomplish during the focus group meeting. It's a good idea to let the group know ahead of time how long you anticipate the meeting lasting. The more of their time they consent to give you, the more creativity you'll be able to draw from them—but it's important that you pace your facilitation to conclude the meeting no later than the appointed time.

The first objective is validation of expectations. Being aware of and responsive to customer expectations is at the very heart of Customer Focus. Many businesses find this difficult because they have no systematic mechanism for discovering just what their customers' changing expectations actually *are* at any given point in time. CFP provides such a mechanism.

Review for the benefit of your customer group each of the expectations within the matrix that were identified during the original CFP session. Apply the following questions to each:

- We assume this is your expectation—is our assumption correct?
- If not, how would you describe your actual expectation?

If the posted expectation is validated as correct, do nothing. If not, remove the erroneous expectation from the matrix and replace it with a fresh Post-it bearing the new, validated expectation written in the customer's own hand.

- What other expectations do you have, if any, which we have not yet captured here?

If any new expectations are identified in response to this question, add them to the matrix. At the conclusion of this exercise, all the expectations posted within the matrix have been validated.

Proceed to the second objective: validation of the Transaction Sequence. Review the posted steps within the matrix.

- Are there any steps posted here that you feel do not belong as part of this type of transaction?

If so, remove these steps from the matrix.

- Are there any additional steps you typically go through as part of this type of transaction which aren't posted here?

If so, add these steps to the matrix. At the conclusion of this exercise, all the Transaction Sequence steps posted within the matrix have been validated.

You're now ready to engage your customer group in the three phases of brainstorming.

For the first phase, draw your group's attention to the first step in the Transaction Sequence.

- What could we do in this first step that would exceed your expectations?

All the ground rules from CFP still apply—participants must, for example, state their ideas aloud before writing them down. The rules of good facilitation still apply as well—no idea is to be dismissed as impractical or inappropriate, participants should be encouraged with generous praise for their ideas, and so on.

Add any and all new ideas to the matrix, then proceed to the remaining steps in the Transaction Sequence. If at the customers' request the meeting is to be kept short, proceed directly to those steps in the Transaction Sequence for which the fewest ideas were generated in the original CFP session.

For phase two, revisit the steps in the Transaction Sequence.

- What could we do in this step that would make you feel important?

Add new ideas to the matrix.

For the third phase, turn the group's attention back to the expectations listed earlier.

- What could we do to better address this expectation?
- How could we ensure that other customers who share this expecation recognize we're addressing this expectation with them in mind?

Add new ideas to the matrix.

The conclusion of the third phase brings the brainstorming activity of the focus group session to an end.

Customers may tend to generate fewer ideas than employees in such a session, but this in no way diminishes the *value* of their ideas. They are providing the most useful form of market research data available—they are virtually spelling out for you what it is you must do to make your business the better alternative in your customers' eyes. The manner by which you choose to express your gratitude should in some way reflect the value you place on the efforts they have made on your behalf.

The critical next step after any focus group session is to reconvene your original participants, review the validated expectations and brainstormed ideas for improvement, add any further embellishments that come to mind, and invite new action initiatives from the team.

It is this cycle—generate ideas, initiate improvements, celebrate successes, soliticit customer involvement and feedback, initiate new improvements, celebrate new successes— that transforms the culture of an organization, that makes workers feel like (and behave like) winners, that allows some businesses to thrive and prosper while competitors flounder and perish.

THE WINNING FORMULA

I'm in a line of work that takes me all over the globe. I've spouted on about customer focus to businesses in Manhattan and in Marrakech, in Hong Kong and Helsinki, in Southern France and Southern Georgia. The currencies may look quite different, the architecture and dress may differ greatly, different languages and different customs— but always the same issues, always the same questions. "Yes, yes, I understand all this, this all makes perfect sense to me, but how do I get my *employees* to see things this way?" In the desert and in the mountains, in great cities and tiny villages, always and forever the same question: "How do I get my workers more motivated?" Everyone understands the complex *mechanics* of their business, while somehow remaining completely in the dark about the most basic *human* elements of business.

And yet, really and truly, it isn't all that complicated. The actual work in most businesses still gets done by people. The better the work these people do, the more successful the business is likely to be. People will not do their best work unless they truly *want* to. This is what "motivation" refers to—they must have a "motive" to work hard, to maintain their concentration, to strive to constantly improve their performance. As their leaders, is there something we can offer these people that will give them such a motive? Yes, indeed there is.

What is the Great Human Motivator? Before you blurt out *money*, stop and reflect with me for just a moment.

Transport yourself back to your first or second job. In those days, even if a shortage of money was a major concern for you, can you truly say this and this alone was your number one motivator on the job? Was it money that drove you to put in those extra hours on that special project that meant so much to you? When you made that painful decision to scrap a lot of the work you'd already done and start over—even though the work was perfectly acceptable—simply because in your heart you knew you could do better, was your decision driven purely and solely by a desire for more money? What about when you made an effort to add a little something extra to work you were doing—even though you knew very well not a living soul would ever notice it—just because *you* knew it was there and it made you feel good because you *cared*; was that for money? Do you remember the time your boss, that really good boss, the best boss you ever had, made that unexpected announcement at the general staff meeting about the something extra you did (which *was* noticed after all) and cited your name and got everyone to applaud, and you could have just died from embarrassment, except now you look back on that as one of the best memories you have of those early days? Funny how stuff like that stays with you over the years, isn't it?

Funny how when we sort through a whole lifetime's inventory of work-related memories and experiences, the ones that always seem to rise to the top are the ones that

represent little moments of personal triumph. We see ourselves standing there, much younger and scrawnier, beam-
ing with satisfaction as someone hands us a plaque or takes
our picture or simply shakes our hand in recognition of
something we accomplished. Suddenly we are *validated*. Our
presence, our passage, has made a difference. Our efforts
have produced some result, and others judge the result to
be good. They approve. Everyone, every living person, seeks
approval; tragically, many are denied it throughout their
entire lives.

Think back to that boss that believed in you, that encouraged you, that sang your praises. Your paycheck may have
been pretty scrawny too back then, but wouldn't you nevertheless have done *anything* for that boss? You were motivated, all right, and not primarily by money. Money can
be a very powerful motivator, but there are others even
more powerful. One of the most powerful of all is *winning*.
Want to get me all fired up? Lay out a challenging assignment for me (win the war in Germany, win the World Series,
win the Baldrige Quality Award, win the Best-Donuts-in-
Town trophy), give me what I need to get the job done, and
keep celebrating my progress as I get closer and closer to
the objective. Make my work feel like play, and I'll play it
for all I'm worth. Treat me like a winner, make me feel like
a winner, and I'll pour everything I have into *being* a winner.
And afterwards, when I've helped your business become
the winning business, the better alternative, I'll actually thank
you for the privilege of letting me be a part of it all.

Customer Focus. Everybody wins. Let's get started.

Snappy Summary

▶ A tidy, orderly CFP matrix invites postsession inspection.

▶ Any session in which more than one participant took on one or more action items calls for a follow-up meeting.

▶ Successes should be celebrated with fanfare and fun in ways that apply the three Customer Focus Principles.

▶ Separate CFP sessions should be considered for each of the key types of customer transactions.

▶ Heads of larger organizations should personally teach team leaders how to facilitate CFP sessions.

▶ Individual successes should be *celebrated*; ongoing patterns of customer-focused behavior should be *rewarded*.

▶ Focus group sessions (patterned on CFP) can spell out what a business must do to become the better alternative.

▶ Winning is a more powerful motivator than money.

▶ In business, Customer Focus is the winning formula.

Index

Other books of interest to you from Irwin Professional Publishing . . .

CUSTOMER CENTERED REENGINEERING

Edwin T. Crego, Jr., and Peter D. Schiffrin

Foreword by Karl Albrecht, author of **Service America!**

This helpful guide presents a comprehensive and tested framework for realigning an organization's strategy, structure, and systems around the customer.

0-7863-0298-4   275 pages

HOW MAY I HELP YOU?

Providing Personal Service in an Impersonal World

Stephen C. Broydrick

No theories or strategies are found in these pages—just techniques that have been tested and proven in the real world of person-to-person contact. Packed with ideas customer service representatives can use immediately, this guide helps create and maintain a competitive edge.

1-55623-989-0   200 pages

(Continued on next page)

OUTSTANDING CUSTOMER SERVICE
Implementing the Best Ideas from Around the World
Colin G. Armistead and Graham Clark

Financial Times Series

A fascinating introduction to service approaches used around the world as well as a detailed plan for developing and implementing your own service strategies.

1-55623-629-8   300 pages

TOTAL CUSTOMER SATISFACTION
Putting the World's Best Programs to Work
Jacques Horovitz and Michele Jurgens Panak

Financial Times Series

Explores the activities of global companies with excellent reputations for customer service. Practical examples and in-depth case studies from the best in the business will enable companies to give customers the best in service quality.

0-7863-0108-2   275 pages